Roland Flade – The Lehmans

Dr. Roland Flade was born September 10, 1951, in Aschaffenburg, Bavaria. He studied history and English at the Julius-Maximilians-Universität (Würzburg), the University of East Anglia (Norwich, Great Britain), and the State University of New York. A newspaper editor since 1979, he has published various scholarly books and numerous articles on past Jewish life in Bavaria. *The Lehmans* is his first book in English. For his work as a journalist and historian, Roland Flade was awarded the Bavarian Constitutional Medal.

Roland Flade

The Lehmans

From Rimpar to the New World
A Family History

Second enlarged edition

Königshausen & Neumann
Würzburg

TO EVA LEHMANN THALHEIMER,
A FIRST COUSIN OF GOVERNOR LEHMAN,
WHO DIED AT TREBLINKA.
SHE IS NOT FORGOTTEN.

Die Deutsche Bibliothek — CIP-Einheitsaufnahme

Flade, Roland:
The Lehmans : from Rimpar to the New World ; a family history /
Roland Flade. – 2., enlarged ed. – Würzburg: Königshausen und
Neumann, 1999
    ISBN 3-8260-1844-3

© Verlag Königshausen & Neumann GmbH, Würzburg 1999
Druck: Verlag Königshausen & Neumann GmbH
Umschlagabbildung: Das Sommerhaus und das
Rimparer Schloß 1845 (Mainfränkisches Museum, Würzburg)
Gedruckt auf säurefreiem, alterungsbeständigem Papier
Umschlag: Hummel / Lang, Würzburg
Alle Rechte vorbehalten
Auch die fotomechanische Vervielfältigung des Werkes oder von Teilen daraus
(Fotokopie, Mikrokopie) bedarf der vorherigen Zustimmung des Verlags.
Printed in Germany
ISBN 3-8260-1844-3

Contents

Introduction

As a German historian and newspaper editor, I have long been interested in the history of German Jews. I am particularly interested in the history of the Jews of Lower Franconia, the northwestern part of Bavaria, where I live.

I vividly remember my first phone conversation with Ambassador John L. Loeb, Jr., in the summer of 1989. He was calling from the Hotel Vier Jahreszeiten in Hamburg and I was sitting at my desk at the Würzburg newspaper, *Main-Post*. When he said he was a relative of former New York Governor Herbert H. Lehman, I immediately recognized that name. During research for my 1985 doctoral dissertation on the Würzburg Jewish community during the nineteen-twenties,[1] I had come across an article on the newly elected governor, published in 1932 by the *Main-Post*'s predecessor. Lehman's forefathers had emigrated from Rimpar near Würzburg to the United States in the middle of the nineteenth century, the article said. The governor regularly visited with German relatives who had stayed behind, the story continued.

None of this, however, went into my dissertation or my next book,[2] published in 1987, dealing with the history of Würzburg's Jews from the Middle Ages to the present. It was this book that Ambassador Loeb bought in a Hamburg bookshop. When he found no mention of Rimpar and the Lehmans, he picked up the phone and called me. Together with his cousin, Wendy Lehman Lash, the ambassador had just organized a Lehman family reunion in New York. From books[3] and family lore, the people congregating in the Lehman Wing of the Metropolitan Museum of Art knew quite a few details about the American history of their family, going back to the year 1844, but almost nothing about its German roots.

Henry, Emanuel, and Mayer Lehman, who emigrated from the small Bavarian village of Rimpar to Montgomery, Alabama, between 1844 and 1850, are personifications of the American success story. From immigrant peddlers and owners of a small "mercantile business," the brothers rose to prominence within less than a decade. Fifteen years after Mayer's arrival in the United States, Jefferson Davis, president of the Confederacy, entrusted him with an official mission. The governor of Alabama spoke of Mayer as "one of the best Southern patriots."

Was there a way of discovering the Lehmans' early history in Germany, Ambassador Loeb asked me on the phone that night. The question triggered a year-long search in Würzburg's State Archives. After going through hundreds of documents, I came up with enough material to put together a skeleton history of the Lehmans' unknown years, which I sent to Mr. Loeb in 1991. This book, *The Lehmans*, is the result of further in-depth research, utilizing material from archives all over the world.

I believe that the story of the Lehman family's German roots is a significant contribution to Lehman family history. There is, of course, no way for me adequately to chronicle the history of the rise of the House of Lehman and its enormous contribution to the American economy and now to the world's economy. The story of the Lehmans' role in financing American business and the participation of hundreds of outstanding men and women involved with Lehman Brothers might take a dozen major books.

I have not written in depth about (and in some cases not mentioned at all) the many outstanding members of the Lehman family besides Herbert H. Lehman, governor and senator from New York. An unusual number of these men and women deserve biographies themselves.

I am deeply indebted to Ambassador John L. Loeb, Jr. Apart from introducing me to the world of the Lehmans, he opened doors for me in Columbia University, where an abundance of material on the governor and his parents is preserved. In addition, he brought me into contact with specialists in the history of the American South. During the development of the book, he proved an ever helpful companion. Patrick T. Lawlor, curator of the Herbert H. Lehman Suite and Papers at Columbia University, and Jaime E. Rodriguez, curatorial assistant, provided hundreds of photocopies pertaining to the life of Governor Lehman and the early days of the family's American history. In addition, Mr. Lawlor was kind enough to give me various scholarly books on the American South unavailable in Germany.

"They kept the records but not the people," Henry Morgenthau III, himself the author of a remarkable book on the history of an important German-American family, quotes a friend who survived Auschwitz.[4] And, indeed, for anybody unfamiliar with the German love for statistics and control, the number of documents about Bavarian Jews still lodged in archives is hard to believe. As often unwanted neighbors, albeit important taxpayers, Jews were traditionally under close scrutiny. Allowing a family to live in a certain place was something that had to be considered very thoroughly. The same goes for the Jews' conduct once they had been admitted. After the ecclesiastical principality *(Hochstift)* of Würzburg, to which Rimpar belonged, became part of Bavaria in 1803, the government wished to find out every last detail about those new subjects. Did the Jews, as was expected of them, really turn from petty trade and money lending to agriculture and handicrafts? What did they teach in their schools? What prayers did they say in their synagogues? Literally millions of pages of reports were written in the nineteenth century alone; statistics were drawn up and questionnaires answered.

During *Kristallnacht* (November 9/10, 1938), SS men and Gestapo officials confiscated an immense number of documents about Jewish congregations in synagogues, Jewish archives, and private homes. While the people whose lives these papers described were cruelly murdered, the documents were brought to Würzburg's State Archives and meticulously filed. Shortly before the end of the Second World War, registers of Jewish births, marriages, and deaths were filmed. The original microfilms perished some time afterward, but copies of those registers survived the war and are now kept in the Würzburg State Archives, together with 19,000 case-files that the Gestapo forgot to destroy.[5] These Gestapo files were created by the police whenever a person was brought to their attention. Some contain an insignificant half-sheet of paper, others run to hundreds of pages. Several thousand Gestapo files deal with Jewish citizens. They are an important source of information on the ordeal of members of the Lehman family during the Third Reich. Dr. Ingrid Heeg-Engelhart and Dr. Herbert Schott were more than generous in providing advice and access to these holdings. Also, Dr. Ulrich Wagner in the Würzburg City Archives deserves my special thanks.

Mayor Anton Kütt of Rimpar gave permission to search through material in Rimpar castle, now used as the town hall. After spending almost a week in the winter of 1989 in a bitterly cold room, I was lucky enough to hold in my hands one single sheet of paper bearing Abraham Lehmann's name. That was the beginning. Mayor Kütt and Christian Will, a former member of the Bavarian Parliament, became enthusiastic supporters of the idea of commemorating the Lehmans of Rimpar, and I am most thankful to both of them.

I had visited the Central Archives for the History of the Jewish People in Jerusalem in 1981 when I wrote my dissertation. I asked by letter for copies of papers from Rieneck, the home of Mayer Lehman's wife Babette; in a short time I received them. Dr. Ursula Gehring-Münzel (Nairobi, Kenya), co-author of my book *Die Würzburger Juden*, was kind enough to send me her transcription of an eyewitness report concerning anti-Jewish riots in 1819.

Prof. Dr. Antonius Holtmann of the Carl von Ossietzky University in Oldenburg found passenger lists of the ships that had brought Henry and Mayer Lehman to the United States in 1844 and 1850, respectively. Prof. Dr. Franz-Josef Eichhorn of the Fachhochschule Würzburg provided me with up-to-date information on the banking firm of Lehman Brothers. Miriam C. Jones, secretary of the Montgomery County Historical Society, and Norwood A. Kerr, reference archivist at the State of Alabama Department of Archives and History, also proved extremely helpful. Henry S. Marks of Huntsville, Alabama, author of a soon-to-be-published book about past Jewish life in Alabama, sent excerpts from his manuscript. Naomi Evetts, archivist at the Liverpool Record Office, collected information on relatives of the Lehmans who had been active in Liverpool and London. Elliott Ashkenazi of Washington, D.C., was kind enough to give me a copy of his brilliant book on Jewish business in Louisiana. This book filled the gaps in my knowledge of the Lehmans' New Orleans activities.

Werner Kleeman, a friend born near Würzburg now living in Flushing, New York, whose life story would be worth telling as well, followed the research and writing of this book with sympathy and valuable hints. Dr. Curt C. Silberman of Florham Park, New Jersey, who personally knew Governor Lehman and took part in the effort to bring relatives of the governor to the United States, shared his memories with me. I also want to express my appreciation to Mr. Arthur G. Altschul of New York. At an early stage of the project, he provided me with information and numerous photographs.

As a German writing in English, I needed the help of someone and found it in the stylistic ability and friendly assistance of Mrs. Cabrini B. Lepis of North Bergen, New Jersey, Mrs. Susan R. Elgart of Plainville, New York, and Dr. Robert Burden of Passau, Germany. Prof. Dr. Herbert A. Strauss, himself a Würzburger, who is now living in New York City, found time in his busy schedule to read parts of the manuscript, and he suggested numerous corrections. Shortly before the book went to the publisher, my American editor, Mrs. Malcolm H. Stern, once again reviewed the manuscript line by line to make it more user friendly to an American audience.

My greatest debt is to my family: my wife, Annette, who made it all possible, and my sons, Lukas and Kilian, who wondered why their daddy had to spend so much time at his desk.

[1] Roland Flade, *Juden in Würzburg, 1918-1933* (Mainfränkische Studien, vol. 34), Würzburg (2nd edition), 1986.

[2] Roland Flade, *Die Würzburger Juden. Ihre Geschichte vom Mittelalter bis zur Gegenwart. Mit einem Beitrag von Ursula Gehring-Münzel*, Würzburg, 1987.

[3] Stephen Birmingham, *Our Crowd. The Great Jewish Families of New York*, New York, Evanston, and London, 1972; Allan Nevins, *Herbert H. Lehman and His Era*, New York, 1963; *A Centennial. Lehman Brothers 1850-1950*, New York, 1950.

[4] Henry Morgenthau III, *Mostly Morgenthaus: A Family History. With a Foreword by Arthur Schlesinger, Jr.*, New York, 1991, p. 6. Mr. Morgenthau, on his mother's side, is a great-grandson of Mayer Lehman.

[5] Herbert Schott, *Ein Staatsarchiv steht nicht außerhalb der Zeit. Faltblatt zur Ausstellungreihe "50 Jahre nach Ende des '1000jährigen Reiches'" im Staatsarchiv Würzburg, Teil 4*, Würzburg, 1995.

Chapter One

The Forebears

It is July 14, 1781. Exactly eight years later, the workers of the Faubourg St. Antoine will storm the Bastille, the royal fortress that commands the eastern side of Paris. The French Revolution will have begun. Twenty-four-year-old Seligmann Löw, the future father-in-law of Abraham Lehmann, is oblivious of these developments. How can anyone in the principality of Würzburg, where Catholic prince-bishops have reigned for hundreds of years, foresee that a revolution, which is about to take place in France, will forever change the face of Europe? Young Seligmann, a Jewish merchant, is very much occupied with his own happiness. He is in love with Edel, a seventeen-year-old girl, and on this fourteenth of July their common future has been decided upon. In his hand he holds a residence permit, a "letter of protection," that enables him to settle in Heidingsfeld near Würzburg. It is his father-in-law-to-be, Edel's father, Meier Lesser, who has secured the letter of protection for Seligmann.

Heidingsfeld as it looked in the 18th and 19th century, before the walls surrounding the town were demolished (Heidingsfelder Flößerzunft)

The Founders

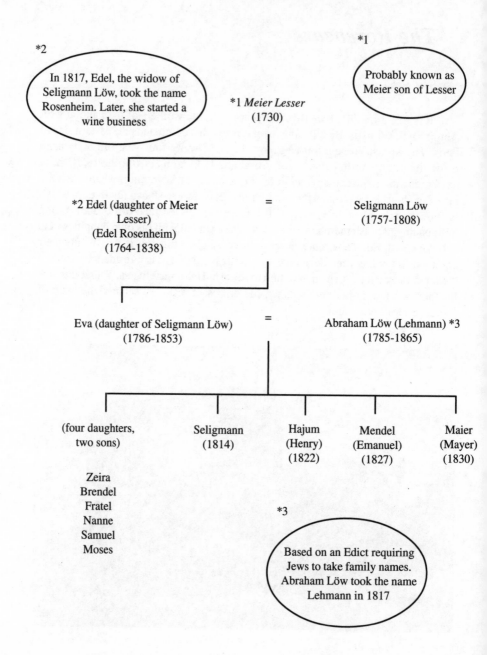

*2

In 1817, Edel, the widow of Seligmann Löw, took the name Rosenheim. Later, she started a wine business

*1 *Meier Lesser* (1730)

*1

Probably known as Meier son of Lesser

*2 Edel (daughter of Meier Lesser) (Edel Rosenheim) (1764-1838) = Seligmann Löw (1757-1808)

Eva (daughter of Seligmann Löw) (1786-1853) = Abraham Löw (Lehmann) *3 (1785-1865)

(four daughters, two sons) | Seligmann (1814) | Hajum (Henry) (1822) | Mendel (Emanuel) (1827) | Maier (Mayer) (1830)

Zeira
Brendel
Fratel
Nanne
Samuel
Moses

*3

Based on an Edict requiring Jews to take family names. Abraham Löw took the name Lehmann in 1817

Germany in the eighteenth century is a patchwork of independent states. The principality of Würzburg is under the control of the Catholic church and is governed by a prince-bishop. These bishops have ruled the city and the surrounding territory since the tenth century and have turned the capital with its 17,000 inhabitants into a center of architecture and the arts, renowned all over Europe for the splendid *Residenz*, Germany's most beautiful Baroque palace. Würzburg is also a center of learning. One year after Seligmann and Edel settle in Heidingsfeld, the university of Würzburg is about to celebrate the two-hundredth anniversary of its founding. Heidingsfeld lies half an hour's walk from Würzburg, up the Main River, surrounded by gentle hills covered with vineyards and fields. Old houses with attached barns and fenced courtyards form solid walls that lean into either side of narrow cobbled streets.

On this June 14, 1781, a representative of the Catholic church has issued Seligmann's letter of protection (*Schutzbrief*), the key document of his future life. Only now is he entitled to live in Heidingsfeld with Edel, to establish a family, and to set about earning his living in an orderly fashion.[1] Residence in a certain community is a privilege, not an absolute right. Seligmann knows that a great number of German Jews are denied this fundamental right of belonging to a place where they can spend their lives. There is a considerable Jewish underclass which does not have permission to live anywhere.

Seligmann Löw's letter of protection, issued in 1781 by the chapter of Würzburg cathedral (Domkapitel) (Würzburg State Archives)

Five years after the American Constitution established complete equality for Christians and Jews for the first time in modern history, Jews in the German states were still suffering from special laws. Seligmann Löw would be a "protected Jew," a *Schutzjude*. The term needs explaining. Jews had been living in what is now Germany since the first centuries of the Christian era. Together with Roman settlers and soldiers, they had come to the Roman provinces of Germania Superior and Germania Inferior. Thriving Jewish communities sprang up in the valley of the Rhine River. Jews were importers and exporters with connections in foreign countries; they were wholesale merchants and moneylenders. For centuries, they lived peacefully among their Christian neighbors. With the first crusade, this quiet life was cruelly interrupted. In 1096, crusaders, on their way to Jerusalem, wrought havoc in Jewish settlements in the Rhine valley. Those Jews who had not been killed, fled.

So it happened that about the year 1100 the first Jews came to Würzburg. The city, however, did not remain quiet for long. In 1147, participants of the second crusade slew twenty-two Würzburg Jews whom they held responsible for the mysterious death of a young Christian man.[2]

The emperors of the Holy Roman Empire [3] realized that Jews needed special protection. Together with women, monks, and itinerant merchants, Jews came under the emperors' custody (hence the term "protected Jew"). However, they were safe only as long as there reigned emperors whose authority was undisputed. When, at the end of the thirteenth century, the empire began to fall apart and prince-bishops and other authorities became responsible for the Jews' safety, most Jews stood alone. Many prince-bishops were more interested in the taxes they collected from their Jewish subjects than in the Jews' well-being.

After 1147, Würzburg's Jewish community turned into an intellectual center of medieval Jewry. The teachings of Würzburg's rabbis were considered essential reading in other, larger, Jewish congregations throughout Europe. This development was brought to an end between 1298 and 1349 by various waves of persecution, motivated by religious prejudices and economic rivalry. The fact that Jews were by now under the protection of the prince-bishop, to whom they paid taxes and who issued their residence permits, could not prevent the murder of nine hundred Jewish men, women, and children in Würzburg in 1298.[4]

After the repeated destruction of Würzburg's Jewish congregation, a new community emerged in the fourteenth century. Jews were now crowded into a few houses at the edge of the city. Fewer and fewer prospects of earning a living were open to them. Generally speaking, German Jews were forced into those professions that Christians were neither allowed nor willing to pursue. Thus, they were pushed to the margins of a society which, at the same time, reproached them for their marginal existence.

In the second half of the sixteenth century, all Jews were expelled from Würzburg. In doing this, the prince-bishops were motivated not only by economic considerations (the protection of the population from presumably fraudulent practices of Jewish traders and moneylenders) but also by the endeavor to restore religious

14

unity in the course of the Counter-Reformation. That is why not only the Jews, but also the Protestants, had to leave.[5] Prince-bishop Julius Echter confiscated the Jewish cemetery and had a hospital, the *Juliusspital*, built on the graves.[6] In addition, Echter founded Würzburg's *Julius-Maximilians-Universität*, that he also named after himself.

The Kapitelhof *in Heidingsfeld before its destruction in the Second World War (Walter Obst, Würzburg)*

Seligmann Löw must have been conscious of the ups and downs of Jewish history in the principality of Würzburg. To be sure, Jews were not allowed to settle in Würzburg itself. But to be permitted to live in Heidingsfeld was acceptable. Seligmann's father-in-law, fifty-one-year-old Meier Lesser, had secured him a place in the Jewish *Kapitelhof*, a small ghettolike housing area consisting of approximately fifteen buildings around a courtyard. Seligmann's family was to live in one of these houses. Many more Heidingsfeld Jews lived outside the *Kapitelhof*, next to Christian neighbors.[7]

In 1781, Heidingsfeld, with more than five hundred Jewish inhabitants, was by far the largest and certainly the most important Jewish community in the principality of Würzburg. The chief rabbi, who was also responsible for ninety-seven other Jewish communities, lived in Heidingsfeld. Since their expulsion from the city of Würzburg more than two centuries earlier, Jews were allowed entrance to the city only during the day and only after they had paid a special tax.[8] Living in Heidingsfeld, within walking distance of the capital, made it possible for Seligmann Löw to do business in Würzburg.

Until the beginning of the nineteenth century, Jewish communities such as the one in Heidingsfeld constituted societies-within-a-society and were endowed with a limited autonomy. Heidingsfeld's chief rabbi administered justice among Jews on the basis of talmudic law. Personal matters like marriage, divorce, and inheritance came under the rabbi's jurisdiction. Jews rarely had social intercourse with non-Jewish neighbors, living out their lives mainly in their own communities.[9] Among themselves, they spoke a language of their own, the so-called *Judendeutsch* ("Jewish German"), consisting of German and Hebrew words written with Hebrew letters.[10]

In 1781, there was a restriction on the number of letters of protection issued. Jewish men often had to wait for years until they were able to acquire one. Christians, however, were suffering from certain restrictions as well. None of the prince-bishop's subjects would have dreamed of marrying when he wanted, not to speak of settling where he saw a future for himself and his wife. In all these instances, documents similar to the one drawn up for young Seligmann were necessary.[11]

There are no existing records to tell us where Seligmann Löw came from. He probably grew up outside Heidingsfeld, as it was his father-in-law who secured his letter of protection and not his own father, of whom we know nothing. Seligmann had to pay ten florin annually for his protection (and that of his future wife), plus twenty florin for his lodgings in the *Kapitelhof*. The right "to carry on an honest trade" went with these taxes.[12]

Despite the lack of personal freedom, Seligmann probably never thought of emigrating. It is no more than a coincidence that Franz Daniel Pastorius, one of Germany's most famous emigrants, had been born in Sommerhausen, some six miles up the Main River from Heidingsfeld. In 1683 Pastorius, together with thirteen families from the city of Krefeld, founded Germantown near Philadelphia, the first German settlement to endure in the American colonies.[13] When Seligmann was a boy, he had witnessed innumerable subjects of the prince-bishop leaving the principality, turning to the Austro-Hungarian Empire, to Prussia, to the North American colonies, and also to Russia, France, Denmark, and Spain.[14] In 1790, when the first federal census was taken, 1,500 Jews lived among the 3.9 million citizens of the original thirteen United States.[15]

We can be quite certain that Seligmann Löw regarded Heidingsfeld as the place where, from then on, he was going to live with his family. Without interruption, Jews had been a part of Heidingsfeld's history since the thirteenth century. After the Jews' expulsion from Würzburg in the sixteenth century, the Jewish congregation had given shelter to dozens, maybe hundreds, of refugees from Würzburg.[16]

Until the middle of the nineteenth century, Heidingsfeld was surrounded by walls. The number of houses within these walls was limited. Thus, the non-Jewish population was often envious when the prince-bishop's officials issued a new letter of protection, enabling another Jewish family to move into a house outside the *Kapitelhof*. As early as 1684, the Heidingsfeld municipal council complained to the prince-bishop's government that young Christian couples had trouble finding homes because there were so many Jews in Heidingsfeld. The complaint was to be repeated regularly during the next century.[17] When Seligmann Löw came to Heidingsfeld, about sixty Jewish families were living in the town.[18]

The interior of the Heidingsfeld synagogue during a sabbath service, shortly after its opening in 1780 (Central Archives for the History of the Jewish People, Jerusalem)

After he was admitted to Heidingsfeld as a protected Jew, Seligmann married Meier Lesser's daughter Edel. The marriage ceremony took place in Heidingsfeld's new synagogue, built in 1780. Illustrations show an impressive house of prayer, erected in the Baroque style, mirroring the faith and the prosperity of this Jewish congregation. Seligmann's and Edel's family grew quickly. In the next two decades, they had eight children: Eva (born in 1786), Klara (1791), Samuel (1794), Babette (1797), a fourth daughter whose name is unknown (1799), Löw (1800), Moises (1802), and Joseph (1805).[19]

While Seligmann and Edel laid the foundation of their family, revolutionary France occupied minds all over Europe. Coalitions were forged, wars fought, territories occupied. In 1796 and again in 1800, French troops marched into Würzburg. After centuries of independence, the principality was reduced to a pawn on Napoleon's chessboard. When Bavaria had to surrender land east of the Rhine to France, it received as compensation the principality of Würzburg in 1803. In the same year, the Bavarian government opened the doors of the city of Würzburg to Jews; a few families were allowed to settle within its walls.[20]

The government was eager to learn how many Jews were living in the newly acquired lands and under what circumstances. A register of the Jewish population of the former principality was put together. For Heidingsfeld, seventy-six protected Jews were listed, together with wives, children, and maids. At this time (1803), the household of Seligmann Löw consisted of himself, his wife Edel, their son Samuel, three daughters, and one Jewish maid. Seligmann's profession was petty trade. His property was worth 4,800 florin; every year he paid 304 florin in taxes. Seligmann's eldest child, Eva, was seventeen in 1803. Since she was not mentioned in the register, perhaps she had gone off to work as a maid with some other Jewish family.[21]

At the beginning of the nineteenth century, almost one in five of Heidingsfeld's 2,720 inhabitants (18.4 per cent) was Jewish. All the others were Catholics. As in Würzburg and many other places, not a single Protestant was allowed to live in the town. The term "petty trade" gives no clue as to the goods Seligmann Löw distributed. It can be assumed, however, that he traveled the country, selling luxury goods, spices, or fancy articles he had brought from fairs in larger cities. From the rural population, he probably bought grain, skins, or wool, thus serving as a middleman between town and country.[22] Seligmann's fortune of 4,800 florin made him a member of the Jewish upper middle class. The average for all seventy-six Jewish households in Heidingsfeld was 3,114 florin, and for all Jewish households in the territory around Würzburg, including the former principality, a mere 1,292 florin.[23]

It must have come as a terrible shock to Edel when Seligmann Löw suddenly died in 1808 at the age of fifty-one. His youngest child had just turned three.[24] Seligmann had to be buried in the cemetery of one of the neighboring Jewish communities because Heidingsfeld's Jewish cemetery was not opened until two years later.[25] Very soon Edel proved that she was up to walking in her late husband's footsteps.

[1] Würzburg State Archives, Statistische Sammlung 616.

[2] Flade, *Würzburger Juden*, pp. 1-5.

[3] The Holy Roman Empire mainly comprised Germanic and North Italian territories. In the Middle Ages, the emperor represented an attempt to maintain ancient Roman traditions of European unity, blessed by a Christian conception of divinely ordained authority, but constant friction with successive popes meant that by the fifteenth century the empire was little more than a legal term for the trusteeship of the German states. A. W. Palmer, *A Dictionary of Modern History, 1789-1945*, Harmondsworth, 1964, p. 155.

[4] Flade, *Würzburger Juden*, pp. 9-29.

[5] Hans-Peter Baum, "Jewish Life in Franconia," in *Genizah. Hidden Legacies of the German Village Jews. An Exhibition by The Hidden Legacy Foundation*, Wien 1992, pp. 33-35; Flade, *Würzburger Juden*, pp. 36-56.

[6] Gravestones that were taken from the cemetery after the destruction of the Jewish community in 1349 were used in other buildings. When one of these buildings, a former Catholic church, was pulled down in 1987, these gravestones were recovered. They are now being studied by Prof. Dr. Dr. Karlheinz Müller of Würzburg University.

[7] The *Kapitelhof* had been bought by the chapter of Würzburg cathedral *(Domkapitel)* in 1628 specifically for the purpose of lodging the Jews under its protection there. The Jews living in *Kapitelhof* paid taxes to the chapter, whereas Heidingsfeld's other Jewish inhabitants were protected by the prince-bishop of Würzburg. Franz Schneider, *Heidingsfeld. Ein altfränkisches Städtebild*, Heidingsfeld 1908, reprinted 1979, pp. 56-57.

[8] Flade, *Würzburger Juden*, p. 58.

[9] Jacob Katz, *Out of the Ghetto. The Social Background of Jewish Emancipation, 1770-1870*, Cambridge, Mass., 1973, pp. 19-20.

[10] Ursula Gehring-Münzel, *Vom Schutzjuden zum Staatsbürger. Die gesellschaftliche Integration der Würzburger Juden 1803-1871* (Veröffentlichungen des Stadtarchivs Würzburg, vol. 6), Würzburg, 1992, p. 27.

[11] This practice continued well into the nineteenth century. Gehring-Münzel, *Schutzjude*, p. 180.

[12] Würzburg State Archives, Statistische Sammlung 616.

[13] Eva Schünzel, *Die deutsche Auswanderung nach Nordamerika im 17. und 18. Jahrhundert*, Würzburg, 1959, pp. 28-49.

[14] Robert Selig, *Räutige Schafe und geizige Hirten. Studien zur Auswanderung aus dem Hochstift Würzburg im 18. Jahrhundert und ihre Ursachen* (Mainfränkische Studien, vol. 43), Würzburg, 1988, pp. 36-42.

[15] H.G. Reissner, "The German-American Jews (1800-1850)," in *Year Book of the Leo Baeck Institute*, vol. 10, 1965, p. 57.

[16] V. Etzel, "Die alte Burg in Heidingsfeld," in *Archiv des Historischen Vereins von Unterfranken und Aschaffenburg*, vol. 69, Würzburg, 1931, p. 39.

[17] Würzburg City Archives, Heidingsfelder Ratsprotokoll 5/234-b, 6/51-a, 6a-136. M. Altenhöfer, *Die Juden in Heidingsfeld. Referat zum Seminar "Die Juden in Franken,"* Sommersemester 1979, Universität Würzburg, p. 4.

[18] Forty of those families lived outside the *Kapitelhof*; Würzburg City Archives, Heidingsfelder Ratsprotokoll 9/603.

[19] Würzburg State Archives, Jüdische Standesregister 40, 41, 111; Gebrechenamt VII W, 154/1606 I; Statistische Sammlung 616; Rosenheim and Lehman family tree (made available by John L. Loeb, Jr.).

[20] Ursula Gehring-Münzel, "Emanzipation," in Flade, *Würzburger Juden*, pp. 61-64.

[21] The reasons that two sons, three-year-old Löw and one-year-old Moises, were not listed remain

unclear. Joseph was to be born two years later. Würzburg State Archives, Gebrechenamt VII W, 154/1606 I.

[22] Gisela Krug, "Die Juden in Mainfranken zu Beginn des 19. Jahrhunderts. Statistische Untersuchungen zu ihrer sozialen und wirtschaftlichen Situation," in Harm Hinrich Brandt (ed.), *Zwischen Schutzherrschaft und Emanzipation. Studien zur Geschichte der mainfränkischen Juden im 19. Jahrhundert* (Mainfränkische Studien, vol. 39), Würzburg, 1987, pp. 47, 70.

[23] Krug, pp. 76, 81.

[24] Würzburg State Archives, Gebrechenamt VII W, 154/1606 I; Jüdische Standesregister 111; Statistische Sammlung 616.

[25] Würzburg City Archives, Heidingsfelder Ratsprotokoll 10/200.

Chapter Two

In the Shadow of the Castle

And now the story repeats itself.

Again a young man comes to the Würzburg region, falls in love with a girl, and tries to find a place where he can live safely with her, earn a living, and raise their children. This man was twenty-two-year-old Abraham Löw, who later called himself Abraham Lehmann. The girl of his choice was Eva, twenty-one years of age, firstborn child of Seligmann Löw and his wife Edel. The place was Rimpar, a small village six miles outside Würzburg; the year was 1807.

In all probability, Abraham Löw and his namesake Seligmann Löw, his future father-in-law, were not related. In the nineteenth century, Löw ("lion") was a common name among German Jews. People called "Löw" lived in almost every Jewish community. Sometimes, their name was spelled "Löb" or "Loeb."[1]

No document tells us where Abraham Löw came from or when he and Eva

Emperor Napoleon and Grand Duke Ferdinand in the park behind the Würzburg Residenz *in 1806 (Sammlung Brod, Universitätsbibliothek Würzburg)*

first met. As a cattle dealer, he may have come across her father, Seligmann Löw, also a merchant, in the course of his daily work. Like Seligmann, he frequented the markets in larger cities, buying cattle that he brought to small rural towns and villages. Jewish cattle dealers often served as a source of cash and credit as well. They bought from peasants in cash and sold to them on credit.[2] It is also possible that Eva, after leaving Heidingsfeld, had worked as a maid with Abraham's father.

Abraham Löw's letter of protection, issued in 1807 by Grand Duke Ferdinand of Würzburg. Later, Abraham Löw changed his name to Abraham Lehmann. (Würzburg State Archives)

Whereas Eva's father Seligmann Löw had encountered little difficulty in being admitted to Heidingsfeld twenty-six years before, it was now almost impossible for a Jewish outsider to settle in the town. The non-Jewish population went to great lengths to prevent any further increase of the Jewish community. Abraham Löw may have tried, but he was sure to fail. Rimpar was different. Only 9.2 per cent of the otherwise exclusively Catholic population was Jewish; there remained room for a young Jewish cattle dealer. On October 29, 1807, Abraham was allowed to settle in Rimpar and marry. The document, however, was not signed by an official of the Bavarian government, as might be expected. What had been the principality of Würzburg for centuries and a part of Bavaria for just three years, had become independent again in 1806 under the name of "Grand Duchy of Würzburg." Two officials of Archduke Ferdinand, grand duke of Würzburg, welcomed Abraham Löw in Rimpar.[3]

The sight of Rimpar in those days must have been a romantic one. The village with its 1,278 inhabitants, among them 118 Jews, was dominated by mighty Grumbach castle and surrounded by hills covered with fields, gardens, and vineyards. In the shadow of the castle stood old farmhouses, timber-framed buildings, and a summerhouse in which the prince-bishops of Würzburg had entertained their guests. It was this summerhouse that caught Abraham's attention upon his arrival in Rimpar.[4]

Those were unsettled times. Until 1814, the former principality of Würzburg belonged to Grand Duke Ferdinand, younger brother of the Austrian emperor, Franz II. Napoleon had removed Ferdinand first from Tuscany and then from Salzburg and established him in Würzburg. In 1806, Napoleon, who had just defeated Austria's and Russia's armies at Austerlitz, turned against Prussia. Many of his troops were concentrated in Würzburg. French officers took up quarters in Rimpar and had to be maintained by the village. Large amounts of food had to be provided as battalion after battalion marched through Rimpar's streets. On October 2, 1806, Napoleon visited Würzburg and spent three days in the *Residenz*. On the early morning of October 6, the successful campaign against Prussia was launched. Many farmers from Rimpar were forced into the army of Ferdinand, Napoleon's ally. Later, they also fought for Napoleon in Spain and Russia. Not long after the Russian campaign had collapsed, Napoleon was driven into exile and the Grand Duchy of Würzburg was again handed over to the Bavarian state. In 1814, Ferdinand left Würzburg and returned to Italy.[5]

By 1810, Abraham Löw - not yet called Abraham Lehmann - had married Eva. Undoubtedly, the ceremony took place in Rimpar's synagogue, which had been erected in 1792. Fourteen Jewish families were counted in Rimpar in that year. They had been accustomed to pray in an attic where it was intolerably hot in summers and much too cold in winters. To make room for the new house of prayer, a barn, owned by a Rimpar Jew, was demolished. The houses to the left and to the right were also owned by Jews; appropriately enough, this part of the village was called Jewish Place (*Judenplatz*). The synagogue, vandalized during *Kristallnacht*, survived the war and is used as a warehouse today.[6] On the outside, a *Chuppastein* (marriage stone) is still visible. It bears the legend "The voice of bliss and the voice of joy. The voice of the bridegroom and the voice of the bride."[7] As was the custom in many German-Jewish congregations, bride and bridegroom broke a glass against this stone after they had been united in marriage.

In marrying Abraham, the cattle dealer, Eva had made a good match. According to a document in the Würzburg State Archives, Abraham Löw's trade capital was 400 florin in 1810 with a probable yearly profit of 100 florin. His property was worth 2,850 florin. This must have been unusual for a man who had just turned twenty-five. Abraham regularly paid taxes such as "protection money" (*Landesschutzgeld*, twelve florin), "new year's money" (*Neujahrsgeld*, two florin), and "extra money" (*Extrageld*, thirteen florin).[8] In contrast to the situations of many of his coreligionists, this should have posed no problem for him.

By settling in Rimpar, Abraham Löw and his wife Eva became part of a Jewish tradition that went back to the second half of the sixteenth century. A Rimpar Jew named Schmul had been mentioned as early as 1577. In 1742, Jehuda ben Isaak Mosche donated to the congregation a so-called *Memorbuch*, which was to keep alive the memory of distinguished members of the Jewish community.[9]

The house that Abraham Löw bought at either the time of his marriage or shortly afterward had been, and now is again, one of the most beautiful in the village;

The summerhouse (left) and Rimpar castle in 1845 (Mainfränkisches Museum,

it was part of a summerhouse originally built in 1600 by Prince-bishop Julius Echter near Rimpar castle. In 1593, Echter had acquired the castle from a member of the Grumbach family. Ten years later, he turned it into a hunting lodge. When Echter entertained guests, he used the summerhouse for banquets and receptions. A high stone wall surrounded the castle compound; when the bishop's guests strolled down from the main building to the summerhouse below, they passed through the park, enjoying beautifully arranged flower beds and a fountain. For almost a hundred and fifty years, the castle with its fifty-four rooms and numerous stables remained one of the most popular country seats of the principality. Echter's successors also loved its atmosphere and used the neighboring forest as a hunting ground. By 1745, however, the prince-bishops had erected a modern country seat in Werneck near Schweinfurt. They lost interest in Rimpar castle, parts of which, notably the western wing, fell into decay and were finally demolished. When the principality, including Rimpar, became part of the Bavarian state, the castle became the property of the Bavarian king, who already had more castles and palaces than he could visit. For a time, the royal forestry superintendent established his office in the castle. In the knights' hall, peas and grain were threshed.[10]

The summerhouse and the park were used to fill Grand Duke Ferdinand's empty coffers. So much money went into Napoleon's lengthy campaigns that Ferdinand had the summerhouse and the adjacent park, by then a mere kitchen garden, sold at public auction on May 15, 1807.[11] Abraham Löw was not among the original buyers because he did not arrive in Rimpar until a few months after the purchase. Some time later, he acquired one third of the house for himself and his family.[12] Today a pharmacist lives and trades in Abraham's home, which has been completely refurbished inside. Nothing reminds a visitor of the family that prospered here almost two centuries ago. Only the solid wooden roofbeams in the attic seem to have been undisturbed during all this time. In commemoration of the Lehman family ancestors who lived there, a plaque is to be unveiled in 1996.

Ten children were born in the house; three of them died at a young age. Before Catholic parish priests started to register Jewish births, marriages, and deaths in 1812, the first child, Zeira, was born. According to an elaborate family tree of the Lehman family, she later married a man named Schloss with whom she had five children.[13] Brendel, the second girl who later called herself Babette, was born on March 12, 1812. She became the wife of a man named Schwab for whom she bore six children.[14] On April 15, 1814, Eva gave birth to her first son, Seligmann, who was named after her deceased father Seligmann Löw. Fratel (born on June 12, 1817), the third daughter, died after three months and was buried in the Jewish cemetery of nearby Schwanfeld, since Rimpar never had a Jewish cemetery of its own. In 1579, Konrad von Grumbach, a nobleman who owned Rimpar and Schwanfeld and various other villages, had given permission to establish a Jewish cemetery in a valley half a mile outside Schwanfeld. At least 2,400 people lie buried there, in what must be one of the most peaceful parts of the region.[15] Jewish visitors from abroad come regularly to Schwanfeld, in search of the graves of their ancestors.

Abraham's and Eva's fourth daughter, Nanne or Nanni (born on March 15, 1820), married a man named Roman with whom she had four sons and two daughters. One of the sons, Seligman (Sigmund) Roman, later emigrated to the United States and, together with his uncles Emanuel and Mayer Lehman, was a director of the Tallassee Falls Manufacturing Company in Tallassee, Alabama, in 1897.[16] On October 7, 1822, Eva and Abraham became parents of Hajum (Chaim), their sixth child. After his emigration to the United States, he called himself Henry. His brother, Samuel (born on September 2, 1825), died half a year later of smallpox. On February 8, 1827, Eva gave birth to Mendel, who became known in America as Emanuel. The ninth child, Maier, was born on January 9, 1830; he was obviously named after Meier Lesser, his great-grandfather. The tenth and last child, Moses, arrived on July 18, 1833, when his mother was forty-seven years old. He died in late August of the same year and was also buried in Schwanfeld.[17]

While the Lehmann family grew, Jewish life underwent basic changes. According to historian Jacob Katz, "the transformation of Jewish society from its prerevolutionary state represents perhaps the greatest upheaval of any sector of European society at that time."[18] Strangers were transformed into citizens. After the city and principality of Würzburg had been returned to Bavaria, the "Edict concerning the relations of the Jews in the kingdom of Bavaria" was introduced to the former principality of Würzburg.[19] Old Jewish institutions were ended. Jews attained a degree of equality before the law unheard of earlier. It was only when the edict became law that the Middle Ages ended for the Jewish population. Rabbis lost all legislative power; Jews were now allowed to possess land, to enter universities, and to choose among a larger number of professions; the way into crafts and into agriculture was opened. However, the edict withheld full civic rights (among others, the right to vote and to serve in the civil service) until an unspecified time when Jews had been "educated" to become "useful citizens," and had been assimilated completely into society. The edict carried clauses to divert Jews from their traditional occupations (trade, money-lending) which had been forced upon them in earlier centuries, and to promote their becoming farmers and handicraftsmen.

There was a limit to the possibilities for integration, however. The edict restricted the number of Jews permitted to live in any Bavarian city or village to the level at the time of its publication by means of a *Matrikelparagraph* (register section), a feature of legislation unknown in other German states. A Polaroid picture, so to speak, was taken of all Jewish communities in Bavaria; the number of Jewish families was to remain unaltered from then on. Before the edict, Jews had been expected to acquire a letter of protection; now they had to be entered into a new register, the *Matrikelliste*. The result was a severe restriction of the Jews' freedom of movement. The register section stipulated that the total number of Jewish families permitted to reside legally in any locality was not to be raised. Therefore, it proved almost impossible for Jewish families to move from villages to larger cities, the unfolding centers of commerce. To make things worse, it was extremely difficult for Bavarian

Jews even to stay in the village in which they had been born. Generally, only the eldest son was matriculated; his younger brothers had to wait until a place on the *Matrikelliste* became vacant through the death of some other person, or because someone had moved away or emigrated.[20]

The edict also determined that all Bavarian Jews were to choose distinctive family names. Until then they had mostly added their father's name to their own, so that Abraham (Ben, son of) Löw probably was the son of a man called Löw. On March 24, 1817, the heads of all Jewish households of Rimpar and of Estenfeld and Veitshöchheim, two nearby villages, congregated in Würzburg and, in the presence of an official of the new Bavarian government, signed a document containing their old and new names. Under number XL we read: "Abraham Löb allda (in this very place, i.e., Rimpar), nun (now) Abraham Lehmann," followed by Lehmann's signature. The signature shows that Abraham Löw (here called Löb) must have been very nervous at this moment. Instead of "Abraham" he put down "Abrabram." Other men were unable to write in Latin letters at all; they put down their names in

On June 2, 1817, Abraham Lehmann and the other heads of Jewish households of Rimpar, Veitshöchheim, and Estenfeld swore the oath of allegiance to the Bavarian king and confirmed the oath with their signatures. Abraham Lehmann's signature is in the fifth line from the bottom of the document in the right column. (Würzburg State Archives)

27

Hebrew letters and had the official authenticate their signatures.[21] It did not take long, however, until, in the course of Jewish emancipation, Bavarian Jews gave up the *Judendeutsch* they had been speaking and writing until then and adopted the German dialect in common with their Christian neighbors.[22]

Why Abraham Löw ("lion") chose Lehmann as his new family name remains unclear. "Lehmann" evokes the word *Lehensmann* ("vassal"), but certainly no German Jew ever had a place within the feudal system. Most popular among German Jews were names with agreeable connotations like Rosenthal ("valley of the roses") or Rosenheim ("home of the roses") or names that indicate the origin of a person ("Kissinger": man from the Bavarian spa Bad Kissingen). In some cases, old names like Seligmann ("blessed man") were retained. According to Benzion C. Kaganoff's *Dictionary of Jewish Names and their History,* "Lehmann," as a Jewish family name, is derived from the profession of banking or money lending. In German, *leihen* means "to lend," *Leihhaus* is a pawnshop, and *Leihmann* was the pawnbroker. This became "Lehmann."[23]

On June 2, 1817, Abraham Lehmann was entered into the Rimpar *Matrikelliste.* The entry mentioned his age (32 years), his profession (cattle dealer), the size of his family (five persons), and his trade capital (600 florin), which had increased by 50 percent within seven years. Interestingly enough, a second Rimpar man, Meyer Jüdlein, chose Lehmann as his new family name. He was two years younger than Abraham. It is impossible to say whether the two were relatives. On the same day, Abraham Lehmann and the other heads of Jewish households of Rimpar, Estenfeld, and Veitshöchheim swore the oath of allegiance to the Bavarian king and confirmed the oath with a second signature. "I (they said, adding their name) swear and repeat this oath: Adonay, one creator of heaven and earth, and of all things, who also created me and all men who stand here, I call you to witness through your holy name, for this time, in truth, that I shall obey the constitution and the laws of the Royal Bavarian State and be loyal to the king, so help me the true God Adonay."[24]

The improvement of the Jews' legal status was extremely unpopular with many Christians. Jews living so long on the fringe of society had been invited by the government to integrate into the mainstream of Bavarian life, and to find new fields of occupation. Christian craftsmen and merchants who had previously enjoyed a monopolistic position, were afraid of Jewish competitors, particularly in Würzburg. Where, for centuries, Jews had not been allowed to stay over night or keep stores, Jewish merchants now bought big houses and hung advertising boards over shop entrances in the busiest parts of town.[25]

Shortly after the Bavarian parliament had discussed (but not decided upon) further reforms in favor of the Jewish population, unrest broke out in Würzburg on August 3, 1819. In the evening, a crowd of hundreds gathered in the streets, abusing Jewish citizens and smashing the windows of Jewish houses and stores. Incidents of looting were reported, but also of courageous intervention by non-Jews. Cries of "Hep-Hep" sounded through the streets, words whose meaning has never been explained convincingly.[26] During the night, Royal cavalry prevented further unrest.[27]

The next day, matters seemed to get out of hand. Advertising boards, the symbols of new Jewish freedom, were torn off all Jewish stores. Jews were followed by angry crowds and had to take refuge in houses; some were mistreated. In various cases, apartments were ransacked. Most Würzburg Jews fled the city, among them Abraham Bing, the chief rabbi. The army was called in to restore peace; this so infuriated a citizen that he shot and killed a soldier through his window.[2b]

Thanks to the determination of the Bavarian king, his government, and the military leadership, the next day was quiet. Sixteen agitators were taken into custody. A government investigation later revealed that Christian merchants were the driving force behind the riot. From Würzburg, the anti-Jewish disturbances spread to other German and European cities, among them Frankfurt, Hamburg, Heidelberg, Copenhagen, and Prague.[29]

The villages around Würzburg were affected, too. In Rimpar, where Abraham Lehmann was living with his wife Eva and two small children, Jewish houses were attacked. In the synagogue, chandeliers and windows were smashed; torah scrolls were torn up and thrown on the street. A local policeman chose to ignore the incident; he was arrested on the following day. A military command of two officers and fifty soldiers was ordered to Rimpar to prevent a recurrence of the unrest. The non-Jewish citizens of Rimpar had to pay for the soldiers' food and lodging as long as they were stationed in the village.[30]

[1] "oe" is another way of writing the German letter "ö" (pronounced as in the French word "feu").

[2] James F. Harris, *The People Speak! Anti-Semitism and Emancipation in Nineteenth-Century Bavaria,* Ann Arbor, 1994, p. 17.

[3] Krug, p. 47; Würzburg State Archives, Regierung von Unterfranken 3137.

[4] Krug, p. 47 (numbers for the year 1803). For a vivid description of nineteenth-century Rimpar cf. Alfons Arnold, *Rimpar im Schein der Fürstenherrlichkeit*, Rimpar, 1965.

[5] Arnold, *Fürstenherrlichkeit*, pp. 161-191; Gehring-Münzel, *Emanzipation,* p. 65.

[6] Arnold, *Fürstenherrlichkeit*, pp. 199-200; Jutta Sporck-Pfitzer, *Die ehemaligen jüdischen Gemeinden im Landkreis Würzburg*, Würzburg, 1988, p. 72.

[7] Christian Will, Werner Siegler, *Das ist Rimpar. Das Arbeiterdorf vor den Toren der Stadt Würzburg,* Rimpar, 1978, p. 179.

[8] Würzburg State Archives, Admin 572/12929 III.

[9] Sporck-Pfitzer, p. 72. A *Memorbuch* often contains memorial prayers and lists of martyrs, communal benefactors, and the like which were read on anniversaries. The name is believed by some to derive from the Latin *memoria.*

[10] Edwin Hamberger, *Das fürstliche Landschloß zu Rimpar im 17. und 18. Jahrhundert* (Mainfränkische Studien, vol. 41), Würzburg, 1987, passim.

[11] Arnold, *Fürstenherrlichkeit*, p. 178.

[12] The exact date of the purchase is unknown.

[13] The children's names were Marcus, Leopold, Clara, Fannie, and Ad(olf?).

[14] Babette's children were called Joseph, Clara (married to a man named Bein), Adelheid (Saltman),

Nathan (married to a woman named C. Frank), Rahel (N. Rotschild), and Nanni (Sichel). From the name of Adelheid's husband it may be inferred that she later emigrated to the United States or Great Britain.

[15] Würzburg State Archives, Jüdische Standesregister 111; Rosenheim and Lehman family tree; *Die Geschichte der jüdischen Gemeinde Schwanfeld*, herausgegeben und gedruckt im Selbstverlag der Gemeinde Schwanfeld, no year.

[16] Virginia Noble Golden, *A History of Tallassee for Tallasseeans,* 1949, p. 42; James L. Loeb, Montgomery, Alabama (letter to John L. Loeb, Jr., September 20, 1995). Nanne's other children were Eva (later married to a man named Rheinheimer), Isaac, David, Elisa (Seaman), and Aron. The name of Elisa's husband indicates that she also emigrated to an English-speaking country, probably the USA.

[17] Würzburg State Archives, Jüdische Standesregister 111; Rosenheim and Lehman family tree.

[18] Katz, *Ghetto*, p. 4.

[19] The edict was promulgated in 1813; it came into effect in the Würzburg region in 1816.

[20] Gehring-Münzel, *Emanzipation*, pp. 71-72; Katz, *Ghetto*, pp. 176, 194; Baum, p. 46.

[21] Würzburg State Archives, Regierung von Unterfranken 3137.

[22] Gehring-Münzel, *Schutzjude*, p. 28.

[23] Benzion C. Kaganoff, *A Dictionary of Jewish Names and their History*, New York, 1977, p. 170. This theory is corroborated by Nelly Weiss, *Die Herkunft jüdischer Familiennamen. Herkunft, Typen, Geschichte.* Bern, 1992, pp. 42, 197.

[24] Würzburg State Archives, Regierung von Unterfranken 3137.

[25] Gehring-Münzel, *Schutzjuden*, pp. 121-133; Jacob Katz, *Die Hep-Hep-Verfolgungen des Jahres 1819*. Berlin, 1994, pp. 23-24.

[26] Probably Gehring-Münzel (*Schutzjude* pp. 134-135) is correct in her assumption that "Hep-Hep" is not supposed to mean anything in particular.

[27] Gehring-Münzel, *Schutzjude*, pp. 136-139; Katz, *Hep-Hep-Verfolgungen*, pp. 14-17.

[28] Gehring-Münzel, *Schutzjude*, pp. 139-142; Katz, *Hep-Hep-Verfolgungen*, p. 31.

[29] Katz, *Hep-Hep-Verfolgungen*, pp. 32-33, 38, 45-49, 57-61.

[30] Gehring-Münzel, *Schutzjude*, p. 146; Katz, *Hep-Hep-Verfolgungen*, p. 52; Arnold, *Fürstenherrlichkeit*, p. 201; Elieser Kraft, Eyewitnes report on the "Hep-Hep" unrests, in Moses Löb Bamberger, *Beiträge zur Geschichte der Juden in Würzburg-Heidingsfeld*, Würzburg, 1905, p. 22.

Chapter Three

Fighting for the Right to Stay

When "Hep-Hep" cries sounded through the city's streets, most Würzburg Jews fled to Heidingsfeld, home of Seligmann Löw's widow Edel and her children. Here the riots broke out on August 4 but did not reach the same peaks of violence as in Würzburg. Elieser Kraft, a Jewish eyewitness, told how Heidingsfeld citizens gave children money to shout anti-Jewish slogans, and how a soldier smashed the windows of two Jewish men's apartments. During the night, Jews patrolled the streets, accompanied by Heidingsfeld's mayor, and peace was finally restored.[1] It was a fragile peace. When Yom Kippur approached, Heidingsfeld's Jews were afraid of another outburst of violence. Younger members of the congregation stood guard outside the synagogue and other houses on the eve of Yom Kippur and during the holiday itself. Again, military assistance was asked for. In many places, fear filled the hearts of Jewish citizens, but no further disturbances occurred.[2]

Heidingsfeld's synagogue (left) and Jewish school (Walter Obst, Heidingsfeld)

Seligmann Löw had been dead for eleven years when the unrest broke out. In 1812, the houses in the *Kapitelhof* had been sold to fourteen Jewish families,[3] one of the buyers being his widow Edel. In 1817, fifty-three-year-old Edel was registered as living in the town with five of her eight children: Samuel (23 years old), Babette (20),[4] Löw (17), Moises (15) and Joseph (12). Eva, the firstborn child, was by now Abraham Lehmann's wife. Klara, the second daughter, had married a man named David Dunkelspiel, with whom she was to have seven children. The girl born in 1799 is mentioned neither in the register nor in the Rosenheim and Lehman family tree; she had probably died before 1817 and was forgotten by later generations.[5]

Even in 1817, Edel's right to live in Heidingsfeld was still based upon the letter of protection bought by her father for her late husband in 1781. Like her husband before her, she traded with (unspecified) goods, but she had added a line of business which was to have a great future in Lower Franconia: wine. As her new name she chose Edel Rosenheim. On September 30, 1817, she was entered into the Heidingsfeld *Matrikelliste* and, together with all the other heads of Heidingsfeld's Jewish families, she swore the oath of allegiance to the Bavarian king.[6] On July 22, 1818, Edel's eldest son Samuel was also entered into the list. By profession Samuel Rosenheim, as he called himself now, was a cattle dealer like his brother-in-law Abraham Lehmann in Rimpar.[7] Samuel played an important role in Heidingsfeld; within a few years he became deputy of Heidingsfeld's Jews *(Judenschaftsdeputierter)*, the man responsible for Jewish-Christian relations and for administering the Jewish congregation's capital. He still held this office in 1843 (or was reelected in that year).[8] Samuel's youngest brother Joseph was thirteen years old in 1818 and, together with sixty-six other Jewish boys and girls, frequented the Jewish school, built close to the synagogue.[9]

Being the widow of a protected Jew, Edel Rosenheim had no difficulty receiving a *Matrikelnummer*. Nor had her firstborn son, Samuel. However, the Heidingsfeld municipal council remained extremely reticent when it came to adding new names to the *Matrikelliste*, even if someone on the list had died or moved away. During the following years, a considerable number of Jewish men were unsuccessful at becoming citizens of Heidingsfeld.[10] Among them were a shoemaker and a watchmaker as well as Edel Rosenheim's second-born son Löw, who, meanwhile, had changed his first name to Leopold.

By 1825, Edel had concentrated her efforts on her wine business, delivering large quantities of wine to customers outside Heidingsfeld. Leopold was responsible for these deliveries and, for that reason, was often away from home. In the summer of 1825, he applied for a *Matrikelstelle* (place on the *Matrikelliste*) and was informed by the municipal council on July 7, 1825, that his application could not be dealt with. There was no way of knowing whether there were any vacant *Matrikelstellen*, a letter said. Leopold complained to the government about the unjust and biased treatment he was receiving. An official advised him to prove to the Heidingsfeld authorities that *Matrikelstellen* were indeed available.

On November 9, 1825, Leopold Rosenheim paid a visit to the town hall with his brother Samuel. The two men presented to the councilors a number of documents which clearly showed that new names could be added to the list without increasing the overall number of Heidingsfeld Jews. Despite this fact the application was refused, ostensibly because Leopold "lacks the necessary capital to operate a wine business." Leopold asked a number of business friends to confirm that his mother's and his wine business was indeed of a considerable size. The correspondents signed a document to that effect, and it was duly presented to the municipal council. The councilors, however, were still not satisfied. They decided that the signatures had to be repeated before their eyes.

One month later, on December 9, 1825, Samuel Rosenheim, acting as representative of his brother, paid another visit to town hall. With him were the signers of the document, except one who was away on a business trip. They were all willing to sign the paper a second time. As soon as they had entered the office, Samuel was shown the door. From the outside, he overheard the men being heavily attacked by both mayor and town clerk. "What!" the mayor cried. "You want to give testimony to the Jew, so that even more Jews are to come to Heidingsfeld? You want to act against the decree of the municipal council?" As the men stood by their decision, the town clerk threatened them with a judicial inquiry. Only then did they agree to delete their signatures or to have them deleted. The mayor or the town clerk even started to cancel the signature of Ignatz Leymeister, a cooper who was absent during the meeting.

After the men had been dismissed, Samuel Rosenheim was called in and presented with the now useless paper. "Gentlemen! This is not the way the document looked when it was handed over to you!" he remarked to the laughing officials. Samuel protested against this kind of treatment and was put under arrest for three hours. On December 22, 1825, he submitted a petition to the Bavarian government. In his letter, he described in full detail the scene in town hall and complained about the municipal council's vicious obstinacy *(boshafte Hartnäckigkeit)*. He implored the government to intervene on behalf of the Heidingsfeld Jews. An investigation into the matter was considered, but evidently never conducted.[11]

One year later, possibly because of Samuel's petition, the Heidingsfeld municipal council changed its mind in the matter. A new application for a *Matrikelstelle* met with a positive reply. Leopold Rosenheim was at last registered as a wine merchant. Earlier, his mother had transferred her wine cellar and her wine casks to him.[12] Edel was sixty-two years old in 1826, and she obviously had to give up her own firm to provide her second-born son with a secure existence. In June 1829, he was married to twenty-four-year-old Mina Segnitz of Gelnhausen (Hesse) by Chief Rabbi Abraham Bing in Würzburg. The couple had four sons, one of whom later emigrated to England (see below).[13] In 1843, Leopold was treasurer of the Jewish community.[14]

In 1828, Samuel Rosenheim and his brother Moritz (formerly Moises) planned to build a vinegar factory in Heidingsfeld. In the municipal council, the project itself was met with approval. It was emphasized, however, that this decision would not influence Moritz's chances for a *Matrikelstelle*, none of which was presently vacant.[15] Even so, Moritz Rosenheim remained in Heidingsfeld. The Jewish Edict made exceptions for factory owners, who were allowed to live in a village or town even when there was no place on the matriculation list. In 1834, Moritz married twenty-three-year-old Philippine Kahn, daughter of a Würzburg merchant.[16] In 1864, after he had given up his business, Moritz moved to Würzburg with his wife. Three years later the couple went to Fürth.[17]

The youngest of the Rosenheim sons, Joseph, also found a way of staying in Heidingsfeld. In 1850, he acted as deputy of Heidingsfeld's Jews.[18] In 1856, he was listed as a wine merchant.[19] Joseph married Jeanette (Nanny) Dunkelspiel, sister of his sister Klara's husband. Two of their six sons emigrated to London.[20]

Samuel, the eldest son of Seligmann Löw and Edel Rosenheim, married three times. According to the Rosenheim and Lehman family tree, he had fourteen children. One of his sons, Seligmann, emigrated to New York. In 1869, he returned to Würzburg where he died in 1914 at the age of ninety-three. One son lived in London.[21] Samuel's daughter, Betty, also spent the last years of her life (until her death in 1905) in Würzburg. One of her sons had emigrated to Liverpool.[22] Johanna, another daughter of Samuel Rosenheim, married the owner of a wholesale firm in textile goods. After his death, she lived in Würzburg as a widow for more than thirty years.[23]

Edel Rosenheim died of apoplexy on March 3, 1838, at the age of seventy-four. The next day, she was buried in the Jewish cemetery of Heidingsfeld,[24] which lay just outside the town's walls and was surrounded by fields. In Würzburg's busy suburb of Heidingsfeld, it is one of the few places of peace and quiet that you can find today. Undoubtedly, Eva Lehmann came from Rimpar for her mother's funeral, together with her husband and her children. Maybe Hajum, Eva's sixteen-year-old son, was already thinking of emigrating when he stood by the grave. He had left school two years earlier[25] and probably had worked with his father, the cattle dealer, ever since. Hajum was only to stay in Germany for six more years.

[1] Gehring-Münzel, *Schutzjude*, p. 146; Kraft, p. 21.

[2] Gehring-Münzel, *Emanzipation*, pp. 80-91; Katz, *Hep-Hep-Verfolgungen*, p. 82.

[3] Altenhöfer, p. 19.

[4] All we know of Babette's later life is that she married a man named R. Oppenheimer; Rosenheim and Lehman family tree.

[5] Würzburg State Archives, Statistische Sammlung 616.

[6] Würzburg State Archives, Statistische Sammlung 616, Regierung von Unterfranken 7136.

[7] Würzburg State Archives, Regierung von Unterfranken 7136.

[8] Würzburg State Archives, Regierung von Unterfranken 8539.

[9] Altenhöfer, p. 17.

[10] Altenhöfer, pp. 9-10.

[11] Würzburg State Archives, Regierung von Unterfranken 7136.

[12] Würzburg City Archives, Heidingsfelder Ratsprotokoll 13, pp. 212-215.

[13] Würzburg State Archives, Jüdische Standesregister 41. Leopold's four sons, Seligmann, Hermann, Meier, and Joseph all founded their own families. Two sons married daughters of their uncle Joseph Rosenheim. Rosenheim and Lehman family tree.

[14] Würzburg State Archives. Regierung von Unterfranken 8539.

[15] Würzburg City Archives, Heidingsfelder Ratsprotokoll 13, pp. 756-757.

[16] Würzburg State Archives, Jüdische Standesregister 41. The couple had six children (Betty, Sigmund, Adelheid, Babette, Lina, and Max). Babette's youngest daughter, Hedwig, married Bernhard Hellmann who, in later years, was a city councilor in Würzburg. Rosenheim and Lehman family tree; Reiner Strätz, *Biographisches Handbuch Würzburger Juden 1900-1945*, I. Teilband, Würzburg, 1989, p. 252.

[17] Würzburg City Archives, Einwohnermeldeamt, Meldebogen Moritz Rosenheim.

[18] Würzburg State Archives, Regierung von Unterfranken 8539.

[19] Würzburg State Archives, Jüdische Standesregister 40.

[20] Their son Julius (born in 1843) moved to Würzburg around 1872 where he lived as a wine merchant and owned a cigarette factory. Sigmund (1839) came to Würzburg even earlier and was co-owner of Julius's wine business. The two brothers married daughters of a Mainz wine merchant. The third son, Max (1849), served in the Bavarian army during the Franco-Prussian war of 1870/71. The sons Wilhelm (1847) and Moritz (1852) emigrated to London in 1878. Nothing is known of the youngest son, Theodor, born in 1856; Würzburg City Archives, Einwohnermeldeamt, Meldebogen Joseph Rosenheim; Strätz, II. Teilband, pp. 475-476; Gehring-Münzel, *Schutzjuden*, p. 271.

[21] Strätz, II. Teilband, p. 476.

[22] The son, Lazarus Fuld, died in Liverpool in 1880 at the age of twenty-three. Strätz, I. Teilband, p. 186.

[23] Strätz, I. Teilband, p. 67.

[24] Würzburg State Archives, Jüdische Standesregister 41.

[25] Würzburg State Archives, Regierung von Unterfranken 8541.

Chapter Four

The Voyage Out

Like his brothers and sisters before him, Maier Lehmann, youngest surviving child of Abraham and Eva, attended the Hebrew school *(Religionsschule)* of Rimpar's Jewish congregation. In the afternoon, Nathan Freund, the Jewish teacher who also acted as cantor in the synagogue, taught religious subjects to a dozen Jewish boys and girls. In the morning, the children frequented Rimpar's Catholic school.[1] We can safely assume, therefore, that Abraham Lehmann's sons and daughters were familiar with the attitudes and customs of their non-Jewish neighbors, maybe more so than the Rosenheims who had gone to an exclusively Jewish school in Heidingsfeld.

Maier's son Herbert H. Lehman later described his father as well-educated. He "must have had a pretty good education," he remembered. These were not empty words. Even forty years after his emigration, Mayer Lehman made surprisingly few mistakes in the German letters he wrote to his son Herbert. Abraham and Eva Lehmann dreamed of a religious career for their son. "His parents hoped that he'd become a rabbi. He was a religious man all through his life," Herbert said about his father in 1957.[2]

Apart from the teacher, another man lived in Rimpar who was indispensable for the observance of Jewish religious law: the ritual slaughterer. The Jews would not eat meat that did not come from properly killed animals. Like most rural Jewish communities, Rimpar had no rabbi of its own. Once in a while, district rabbi Abraham Bing and his successor Seligmann Bär Bamberger came from Würzburg to look after the congregation. In the rabbi's absence, the cantor was responsible for singing the appropriate prayers during service, sometimes accompanied by the congregation. Services took place twice a day during the week (in the morning and in the evening). On sabbaths and holidays, there was a third service in the afternoon. At least once every week, a prayer for king and government was said.[3]

Although they obviously had no need for the Catholic parish priest, the twenty-six Jewish families of Rimpar had to pay thirteen florin annually to him. Twelve florin went into the maintenance of the Jewish cemetery in Schwanfeld, 212 florin into the Jewish school (with the teacher receiving a salary of 170 florin), and forty-five florin into the Christian school. To balance the Jewish congregation's budget, every adult member had to contribute money according to his fortune. Among the many taxes Rimpar's Jews had to pay was the poll tax *(Leibzoll)* for every person buried in Schwanfeld.[4]

There seems to have been an atmosphere of tolerance in Rimpar which, within the limits set by the Jewish Edict, made life easier than in, say, Heidingsfeld. The Jewish population of Heidingsfeld decreased from 500 to 319 between 1813 and 1847. We may well be right in attributing this development partly to the anti-Jewish stand of the councilors and some of the non-Jewish citizens. In Rimpar, on the other hand, the number of Jews rose slightly, from 118 in 1813 to 122 in 1848.[5] Although twenty-five Jews emigrated from Heidingsfeld to the United States between 1843 and 1847, there are no Rimpar emigrants known for those years, apart from Hajum (Henry) and Mendel (Emanuel) Lehmann, of course.[6]

When, in 1833, the Bavarian government asked for yet another detailed report about Jewish life and Jewish expectations, the official responsible for Heidingsfeld and some neighboring Jewish communities sent in a noncommittal answer, culminating in the patently false statement, "The Israelites have no complaints." His colleague, reporting about the Jewish communities of Rimpar, Veitshöchheim, and Estenfeld, took great pains to paint a more realistic picture of the Jews' situation. In doing so, he did not spare his Christian coreligionists. His report is an impressive example of unbiased thinking and deserves to be quoted in detail. "There are those people who charge Jews with their ruin," wrote the government official. "Upon impartial examination, these complaints turn out to be completely or mostly unfounded," he continued. Quite to the contrary: "Jewish artisans should serve as an example to all Christians." Jewish merchants, in the author's eyes, were indispensable for many people's well-being: "Jews trade in goods and especially in cattle and they advance cash. Where no Christian will lend money, the Jew still grants a credit. Many families would go hungry without the cow borrowed from the Jew. ... Those families who claim to have been ruined by Jews would, without Jews, only have been ruined earlier. Jews are quiet, law-abiding subjects, peaceable citizens, in every respect thrifty and sober, assiduous and hard-working. ... They are charitable towards their own and other poor. Their whole life is exemplary, their learning superior to most country people. ... For many years, no Jew has been punished for crimes or offenses, something that happens very often with Christians."[7] Abraham Lehmann, the cattle dealer, may well have been among the models that occasioned this glowing description of the Jews of Rimpar, Veitshöchheim, and Estenfeld.

It comes as no surprise that the author suggested far-reaching improvements of the Bavarian Jews' legal status, steps that actually were to be taken only three decades later. "Everybody will understand that circumstances cannot remain as they are now," he wrote, unable to imagine that the *Matrikelparagraph*, to name but one example, was to remain in effect until 1861. Why not try "complete emancipation of the Jews," the official asked, pointing to other countries where Jews had already been emancipated. It was high time, he emphasized, to make Jews "real members" of the state and not regard them as strangers and intruders any longer.[8] Certainly these were the hopes of Abraham Lehmann and his children as well. The obvious fact that Bavaria was unwilling to offer its Jewish citizens equal opportunities, however, made the children think twice about staying, as their uncles Rosenheim had done. The Rosenheims' degrading fight for the right to live in Heidingsfeld could not, despite their eventual success, serve as an example for the Lehmanns. Having lost most illusions about Bavaria, they found that emigration to the United States of America had become a very real possibility during the last decades.

In 1819, the American paddle wheeler *Savanna* was the first steam-driven vessel to cross the ocean. It made America seem wonderfully accessible. Soon a great migratory move westward to "the land of freedom and enlightenment, the land moreover of land and money" (as Stephen Birmingham has graphically described it[9]) had begun. For the first time, northern Bavaria was affected considerably by emigration to the United States. In 1829, Gottfried Duden, a German graduate in law and medicine, who had settled in the newly opened Missouri territory five years earlier, published his *Report on a Journey to the Western States of North America*. Duden depicted the vast spaces and the democratic life of America and compared both with the social and political pressures that the individual had to bear in Germany. Other books in the same vein followed soon.[10] The *Allgemeine Zeitung des Judentums*, a periodical which began to appear in 1837, reported continuously about groups of Jewish emigrants who had left for America, and about their fate.[11] It is not improbable that these books and articles were also read in Rimpar.

In the thirties, it became much easier to reach German and other seaports. Tolls and restrictions on navigation on rivers like Main or Rhine were cleared away. In 1842, Main river steamers began operating from Würzburg.[12] At the same time, trade between Bremen and American ports grew. Ships, mostly sailing ships, bringing cotton and tobacco from Baltimore and New Orleans, lacked freight on their outward voyage. Who could better fill the *Zwischendeck* (steerage) than American-bound emigrants?[13] In growing numbers, enterprising young Jews left their villages and went to America, the "land of freedom, where the name Jew and the accidental fact of having been born a Jew is nobody's ruin," as Würzburg's Jews reported to the government.[14]

Leopold Sonnemann, who later founded the famous liberal newspaper *Frankfurter Zeitung*, witnessed numerous emigrations during the 1830s. Sonnemann, son of a Jewish weaver, lived in Höchberg near Würzburg, another of those villages where Würzburg Jews had settled after their expulsion. "After some pioneers had gone forward and made rapid progress during their first years in the United States," Sonnemann wrote in his memoirs, "emigration became a mass phenomenon. It was then that those numerous Bavarian Israelites went to America who are rich and respected today. On one day eight or nine young folks from the small village of Höchberg took their leave together, probably the most skillful and vigorous elements of the population. I remember vividly how they said good-bye in our yard on a beautiful summer evening. The voyage to America on a sailing-ship took about six weeks in those days. To the inlander, the trips seemed like what a North pole expedition would be today. Soon the emigrants sent more or less favorable reports, in some cases accompanied by bills of exchange for 100, 200 and 500 florin, money to pave relatives the way to the USA. After a few years America was praised as the dorado of energetic young people."[15]

Even then, however, there were those who rejected the idea of going to America on ideological grounds. Gabriel Riesser, later to become influential during the abortive German revolution of 1848, deplored the reactionary yoke weighing upon German Jews, but continued in a letter written in 1838: "The thought of emigration to America has seized many of the best, and several hundred Jewish families have already gone through with it in the last few years. I could have taken up this thought with enthusiasm, had not America disgusted me recently with slavery, the status of the free colored people and all the atrocities which result from these evils."[16]

Many emigrants from Southern Germany went to the Low Countries' ports and Le Havre in France, cities that were more easily and cheaply accessible than Hamburg and Bremen. Bremen's port, Bremerhaven, had only been opened in 1830, and the city actively sought to attract emigrants. In 1832 and 1834, special laws aimed at decent treatment for emigrants were passed. Inns were inspected, and ships were required to provide sufficient space and food. By 1836, Hamburg, whose commerce was already well established, also opened its doors to emigrants, whose humane treatment, however, was not the city government's primary concern. Only in 1845, when the volume of emigration began to swell and Hamburg's share remained small compared to Bremen's, regulations were strengthened.[17]

Between 1835 and 1837, more than 3,500 Christians and Jews from the governmental district of Lower Franconia (largely identical with the former principality of Würzburg) sailed to America. From 1838 to 1840, another 5,000 Lower Franconians went to the United States.[18] Many of them, however, were being cheated by dubious emissaries of shipping companies and by unreliable agents who had only their own profit in mind. Thus, in 1840, Bavaria began to licence its own agents, who were to be kept under close surveillance. Only solvent commercial houses were to be considered, the government decreed, houses whose business was so substantial that there would be no need for enticing subjects of the king away from home. Within seventeen months, twelve agents of shipping companies in Bremen and Hamburg were licensed in Lower Franconia alone. In March 1842, Dr. Strecker of Mainz, the only agent not living in the governmental district itself, became a Bavarian agent for emigrations via the French port of Le Havre.[19] Shortly afterward, Hajum Lehmann must have turned to this man to learn how to get to the United States.

Numerous Bavarian Jews had made such a step before him. Adam Gimbel, born in 1817, left Bavaria for New Orleans in 1835, peddled up and down the Mississippi river valley and opened a dry goods store in Vincennes, Indiana. Out of it grew the Gimbel Brothers chain of department stores. Joseph Seligmann of Baiersdorf climbed on a horsedrawn wagon in 1837 with eighteen other Baiersdorf boys. The trip to Bremen took seventeen days. They camped along the roads at night. Joseph also went to the American South, where he peddled his wares with various brothers and sisters. In 1864, the merchant and investment banking firm, J. & W. Seligman & Co., was founded. Benjamin Blumenthal of Bavaria arrived in New York in 1837. His sons, Lyman and Joseph Bloomingdale, opened the Bloomingdale Brothers Department Store in 1886.[20]

On May 7, 1841, Michael Stein of Weickersgrüben in Lower Franconia paid 312 florin for the passage to America to Joseph Maier Kohnstamm, the agent of a Bremen shipowner.[21] In her novel *The Making of Americans,* Michael's granddaughter Gertrude Stein vividly described how difficult it was for him to leave the mother country behind.[22] Together with his wife and four children, among them

Gertrude's father, Michael Stein boarded the bark *Pioneer* in Bremerhaven, and it arrived at Baltimore on September 2, 1841.[23] Emigration dealt a severe blow to the Jewish community of Weickersgrüben. In 1833, fifty-five Jews in eleven families had been counted.[24] In 1854, after three families with twenty-three members had emigrated to the United States and others had moved away, there remained only six housholds, consisting of one family of four persons, two widows with twelve dependents, and three unmarried persons with another three dependents.[25]

Steerage passengers on an emigrant ship on their way to America
(Schiffahrtsmuseum Bremerhaven)

In 1843, fourteen-year-old Levi Strauss of Bavaria sailed from Bremerhaven to New York, where his two elder brothers had already established a wholesale textile and tailoring business. Strauss went on to California and became world famous by creating durable work trousers out of canvas.[26] In 1839, the *Allgemeine Zeitung des Judentums* published a letter from Würzburg complaining about the considerable Jewish emigration: "If the present tendency is to continue, numerous small communities will be compelled to close their synagogues and schools. They will not be in a position to pay their teachers and synagogue personnel unless the state comes to their aid. In many a place, out of a Jewish population of thirty to forty families, fifteen to twenty people have emigrated, mainly the young and employable."[27]

From passenger lists of emigration ships we learn that unmarried emigrants like Adam Gimbel, Joseph Seligmann, and Levi Strauss were far more numerous than married ones. To vacate a *Matrikelstelle*, as Michael Stein did, was a rare event. Most of the people leaving for overseas decided to emigrate precisely because they had failed to obtain one or saw no chance of being matriculated (and permitted to marry) within a reasonable span of time.[28]

Twenty-one Jews emigrated from Rieneck, another small village near Würzburg, between 1830 and 1854, eighteen of them to North America. Rieneck was the place where Benjamin Neugaß, a weaver, was allowed to settle in 1835. At least four of Benjamin's children later went abroad, among them Babette who became the wife of Maier Lehmann. Almost all of the Rieneck emigrants were single; eight of them explained their emigration with the fact that they had not been accepted on the *Matrikelliste*.[29]

Hajum Lehmann, twenty-one years old and single, fitted well into this pattern when he left Rimpar and his family in the summer of 1844. In that year alone, 1,850 men, women, and children from Lower Franconia took this step.[30] Probably Hajum first traveled by steamboat on the Main River to Mainz, a journey which normally lasted one and a half days.[31] In Mainz, he must have boarded another steamboat traveling on the Rhine to Rotterdam. There he had to take yet another ship for Le Havre, where the *Burgundy* may already have been waiting for him and other emigrants.

We can only guess what befell Hajum and the other steerage passengers on their voyage. Being a young man, he may not have suffered as did older emigrants or parents of young children from cramped conditions, monotony, darkness, and filth on board. Seven boys and girls from five to eighteen years traveled with Conrad Goehring, a farmer from Württemberg, and his wife Agnes. Israel Serguet and his wife Henriette from Switzerland had three children with them, one of whom, Emile, was just nine months old.[32] Hajum probably witnessed storms, deaths, and burials at sea. Joseph Seligmann, who had sailed as one of 142 steerage passengers to New York seven years before, later described his voyage with the words "The less said about it the better."[33] We know, however, that on some ships dance and song kept up the emigrants' optimism and helped to create a spirit of togetherness aboard.

On September 11, 1844, Hajum Lehmann set foot on American soil in New York harbor. From then on he was Henry Lehman.

---

[1] Würzburg State Archives, Statistische Sammlung 279, Regierung von Unterfranken 8541; Arnold, *Fürstenherrlichkeit*, p. 201.

[2] *The Reminiscences of Herbert H. Lehman*, Oral History Research Office, Columbia University, New York, 1961, 1969, p. 10.

[3] Würzburg State Archives, Statistische Sammlung 280.

[4] One florin and fifteen ducats for a "big corpse" (*große Leiche*), 37.5 ducats for a "small corpse" (*kleine Leiche*); Würzburg State Archives, Statistische Sammlung 280.

⁵ Krug, p. 47; Würzburg State Archives, Regierung von Unterfranken 8540, 8515.

⁶ Würzburg State Archives, Regierung von Unterfranken 8515.

⁷ Würzburg State Archives, Statistische Sammlung 280.

⁸ Ibid.

⁹ Birmingham, p. 21.

¹⁰ Klaus Wust, Heinz Moos (eds.), *Dreihundert Jahre deutsche Einwanderer in Nordamerika. 1683-1983. Ihre Beiträge zum Werden der Neuen Welt*, Gräfelfing (2nd edition), 1983, p. 40.

¹¹ Reissner, p. 71.

¹² One of the founders of the *Maindampfschiffahrtsgesellschaft* was Joel Jakob von Hirsch, a member of Würzburg's most distinguished Jewish family. Gehring-Münzel, *Schutzjude*, pp. 222-223.

¹³ Wust, Moos (eds.), p. 40; Mack Walker, *Germany and the Emigration 1816-1885*, Cambridge Mass., 1964, p. 46.

¹⁴ Gehring Münzel, *Emanzipation*, p. 116.

¹⁵ Quoted in Heinrich Simon, *Leopold Sonnemann. Seine Jugendgeschichte bis zur Entstehung der Frankfurter Zeitung*, Frankfurt a.M., 1931, pp. 15-16.

¹⁶ H. G. Reissner, pp. 64-65. Cf. Bertram Wallace Korn, "Jews and Negro Slavery in the Old South, 1789-1865," in Leonard Dinnerstein, Mary Dale Palsson (eds.), *Jews in the South*, Baton Rouge, 1973: "The lot of a free Negro was far from simple; his choice of mates was extremely limited. Most frequently he had to buy his own woman, and unless he could emancipate them, which was next to impossible, he was compelled also to own title to his own children" (p. 120).

¹⁷ Walker, pp. 87-92.

¹⁸ Marianne Wellhausen, *Über deutsche Auswanderung nach den Vereinigten Staaten von Nordamerika im 19. Jahrhundert, unter besonderer Berücksichtigung Mittelfrankens*, Phil. Diss., Erlangen, 1949, pp. 50, 91.

¹⁹ Würzburg State Archives, Regierung von Unterfranken 9372.

²⁰ Birmingham, p. 22; Reissner, pp. 109-110.

²¹ Würzburg State Archives, Regierung von Unterfranken 9372.

²² Gertrude Stein, *The Making of Americans. Being the History of a Family's Progress.* New York, 1925, reiss. New York, Frankfurt a.M., Villefranche-sur-Mer, 1966, pp. 36-41.

²³ The National Archives of the United States, National Archives Microfilm Publications, Microcopy no. 255, *Passenger Lists of Vessels Arriving at Baltimore 1820-1891*, Roll 3.

²⁴ Würzburg State Archives, Statistische Sammlung 279.

²⁵ Central Archives for the History of the Jewish People, Jerusalem, WR 15.

²⁶ Wust, Moos (eds.), p. 139.

²⁷ Rudolf Glanz, "The Immigration of German Jews up to 1880," in *YIVO Annual of Jewish Social Sciences,* vol. 2-3, New York, 1947, p. 90.

²⁸ Jacob Toury, "Jewish Manual Labour and Emigration. Records from some Bavarian Districts (1830-1857)," in *Year Book of the Leo Baeck Institute,* vol. 16, 1971, p. 60.

²⁹ Central Archives for the History of the Jewish People, Jerusalem, WR 15; Würzburg State Archives, Statistische Sammlung 617.

³⁰ Wellhausen, p. 91.

³¹ Würzburg State Archives, Regierung von Unterfranken 9372.

³² The National Archives of the United States, National Archives Microfilm Publications, Microcopy no. 237, roll 56.

³³ Birmingham, p. 22.

Chapter Five

The Immigrants' Progress

Before the middle of the nineteenth century, New York harbor at the southern end of Manhattan Island was probably the most vibrant port in the world. Steam-driven ferries traveled to Brooklyn and Hoboken. Rowboats with two or three oarsmen and somewhat larger sailboats swarmed around incoming ships, ready to take aboard passengers who were unwilling to wait until their ship had docked. Reporters hungry for foreign news came onto the ship, accompanied by merchants and innkeepers offering overnight accommodation. After monotonous weeks on the ocean, many immigrants were shocked by the hectic scene surrounding them.[1] "Where is the pen to depict what we saw, to describe what we felt?" twenty-one-year-old Friedrich Gerstäcker from Germany wrote to his mother after he had reached New York on an emigrant ship in 1837. "Delicious was the sight of the land shining in fresh green, with lush forests and splendid houses, with forts to the right and left, protecting the harbor, above us a friendly blue sky, beneath us softly murmuring waves."[2]

America was young in 1844. Just twenty-five years earlier, Alabama had entered the Union as its twenty-second state; Maine, Missouri, Arkansas, and Michigan had followed during the next quarter of a century. Around twenty million people lived in those twenty-six states.[3]

Henry Lehman's journey, of course, was far from over. Unlike many immigrants, he did not stay in the industrialized northern states. Coming from rural Bavaria and a family of cattle dealers and wine merchants, it seemed only natural to move southward after the ocean passage. He boarded a ship (packets ran monthly between New York and Mobile, Alabama[4]) and sailed along the eastern coast, passing Virginia, the Carolinas, and Georgia. After he had sailed around Florida, which was to enter the Union one year later, Henry finally arrived at the port city of Mobile some time during the fall of 1844.

What drove Henry Lehman to Alabama, of all places? Had he heard of its thoroughly rural character? Even in 1850, only ten places had as many as a thousand people.[5] Agriculture was Alabama's primary interest before the Civil War, "King Cotton" being its chief source of wealth. Most of the people worked on farms and plantations. Towns and cities came into existence to supply the agricultural needs of the state and to process and distribute farm commodities.[6] The American South in antebellum days offered Jewish immigrants an agrarian structure similar to that back home. To cater to farmers' needs was definitely something that Henry had learned back home.

Had Henry any idea of the flourishing cotton trade in Alabama? Cotton in itself was a familiar commodity in Bavaria. Numerous cotton weavers, many of them Jews, were active in Rimpar and the surrounding villages. Actually, weaving, tailoring, butchering, and shoemaking were the preferred Jewish crafts.[7] Mobile, situated on the Gulf coast, was the very harbor from which bales of cotton had been and still were being shipped to Germany. With over 12,000 inhabitants, the city was by far the largest settlement in Alabama, whose population had risen to almost 600,000 by 1840.[8] "Mobile is a place of trade, and of nothing else; the quays are crowded with shipping, and in amounts of exports it is inferior only to New Orleans," a traveler observed.[9]

Slaves loading bales of cotton onto a steamboat on the Alabama River (State of Alabama Department of Archives and History, Montgomery)

Did Henry Lehman go to Alabama because people he knew, specifically members of the Goldschmidt family of Heßdorf, had already established themselves there? It may be a coincidence that two young men from Bavaria named Goldschmidt (Meyer Goldschmidt, twenty-four years old, and Arnold Goldschmidt, eighteen years old) were among the steerage passengers on the *Burgundy's* trip to New York.[10] There are no documents left to tell us whether those two came from Heßdorf, a small village some fourteen miles north of Rimpar.[11] This may, however, very well be the case. We know for sure that a Heßdorf man named Lewis Goldsmith (originally Goldschmidt) had arrived in America in 1837, when he was about twenty-six years old.[12] In 1844, the very year Henry Lehman turned up in Mobile, Lewis Goldsmith ran a wholesale clothing firm in that port city; his principal customers were Jewish peddlers and rural storekeepers. Around 1846, Goldsmith moved to New Orleans.[13] In 1848, Henry's brother Seligmann, who stayed in Rimpar, was to marry a girl from the Goldschmidt family of Heßdorf. This girl's sister, incidentally, was the mother of Babette Neugaß, who became Mayer Lehman's wife a decade later. Mayer first met Babette at Seligmann's wedding and again in the Goldsmiths' house in New Orleans, where she visited relatives.

In Mobile, Henry Lehman witnessed steamers running on the Alabama River toward the state's capital, Montgomery. Grain, flour, meat, lumber, liquors, tobacco, and every possible sort of household item and luxury found their way up the river to consumers. The trip between the two cities took two days.[14] The state's economy was expanding fast and Henry wanted to be part of it. He bought goods that he knew farmers needed and set out as an itinerant merchant along the highways and byways of Alabama, slowly moving north. Whether he carried his merchandise in a pack on his back, or used a wagon right from the start, does not make much of a difference. With Henry peddling his way, just as had his grandfather Seligmann Löw, the *Kleinhändler*, the Lehman family had come full circle.

Peddling, in those days, forced an immigrant to become familiar with a particular territory and its inhabitants. To young and adventurous men like Henry Lehman, peddling in a thinly populated area with poor internal communication and transportation proved a challenge.[15] In his memoirs, Oscar Straus, also of Bavarian origin, described the life of Jewish peddlers in the South in the middle of the nineteenth century. He summed up the recollections of his father, Lazarus Straus, in this way: "The itinerant merchant ... filled a real want, and his vocation was looked upon as quite dignified. Indeed he was treated by the owners of the plantations with a spirit of equality that it is hard to appreciate today. This gave to the white visitor a status of equality that probably otherwise he would not have enjoyed to such a degree. Provided only, therefore, that the peddler proved himself an honourable, upright man, who conscientiously treated his customers with fairness and made no misrepresentations regarding his wares, he was treated as an honored guest by the plantation owners, certainly a spirit of true democracy."[16]

Within a year, Henry arrived in Montgomery. Six thousand people were then living in this town on the left bank of the Alabama River, among them two thousand slaves. The state capital had been founded only twenty-five years earlier. Wooden houses and livery stables lined unpaved and unsanitary roads. Swarms of flies filled the air. Yellow fever was endemic. Henry Lehman may have had an inkling of Montgomery's big future, though. Linked to the ports of both Mobile and New Orleans, Montgomery was a natural storehouse and center of the flourishing cotton trade. After a year on the road, Henry settled down. He rented a frame house on Commerce Street and laid out his meager stocks of general merchandise on bare shelving: crockery, glassware, tools, dry goods, and seeds. Outside his little shop he hung a sign bearing the legend *H. Lehman*.[17]

Henry lived in the back rooms, working far into the night by the light of candles and lamps fueled by whale oil. It was a lonely existence, and he never lost his fear of yellow fever. In a letter to Rimpar he wrote of the considerable business opportunities in Montgomery, "if the fever doesn't get me first."[18] There is room for another enterprising young man, he must have added. Mendel, Henry's junior by five years, heeded the call. Whether Henry also invited his sisters, who had probably married by now, is an open question. After they had gained a foothold, many young immigrants made arrangements for brothers and sisters to follow them. Actually, this "pulling after" of relatives was the most significant feature of German-Jewish immigration to America.[19]

While Henry Lehman was establishing himself in Montgomery, Bavarian Jews started another attempt for full equality. In petitions to Parliament they argued that they performed equal duties and should have equal rights. Specifically, they took issue with their exclusion from state service. In April and May of 1846, Parliament debated the matter and passed a proposal requesting the king to submit draft legislation for the repeal of laws restricting the Jews. However, it took two years until the Ministry of the Interior responded and began to put together a bill for revision of the Jewish Edict.[20]

By that time, Mendel had already reached America. Together with 3,073 Lower Franconians[21] he crossed the Atlantic in 1847. Due to food shortages in many parts of Germany, caused by repeated crop failures, emigration from Germany, after fluctuating around 20,000 a year for a decade, rose sharply to four or five times that number in 1847.[22] Emanuel Lehman, as he came to call himself in America, joined his brother in Montgomery. Awaiting him was a ready-made "mercantile business." One year later, Henry and Emanuel moved their shop to a two-story wooden house at 17 Court Square. A new sign (H. Lehman & Bro) went up. Eventually, the partners bought the corner plot in the heart of town.[23]

Almost nothing is known of the young men's private lives during the first years of their Alabama existence. On November 5, 1849, Henry, who was twenty-seven at the time, married a woman named Rosa Wolf, obviously also of German descent, in Montgomery.[24] Within the next six years, four children (David, Bertha, Harriet, and Meyer) were born.[25]

The year 1848, by the way, saw the emigration of two Lower Franconian Jews whose names, like Lehman Brothers, are famous today in the world of investment banking. Joseph Sachs, the scholarly son of a saddle maker, had grown up in a village near Würzburg. When he fell in love with the daughter of a Würzburg goldsmith and her parents disapproved, the couple eloped to Rotterdam where they married and boarded a ship to Baltimore. In the same year, Marcus Goldman, a twenty-seven-year-old man from Burgpreppach, arrived in New York. Like so many other Jewish immigrants he started out as a peddler (in Pennsylvania) and then turned to banking in New York. Joseph Sachs's eldest son Julius, a scholar like his father, later founded the Sachs Collegiate Institute in New York, which was frequented by many children from German-Jewish families. The second son, Sam, married Marcus Goldman's daughter Louise and became the first partner in Goldman's commercial-paper business.[26] Today, Goldman, Sachs is one of the most prestigious investment banking firms in America.

German Jews had appeared in North America in small numbers early in the eighteenth century. In 1733, a group of forty arrived in Savannah, Georgia. The first German-Jewish congregation was established in Philadelphia in 1780.[27] Five years later, a Jewish man named Abraham Mordecai was among the first settlers in

Montgomery County.[28] By 1840, about 15,000 Jews were living in the United States at large and just a few hundred in Alabama,[29] compared to 16,451 in Lower Franconia alone.[30]

No Jewish community was there to embrace Henry Lehman upon his arrival in Montgomery. In Rimpar, he had left a well-established *Gemeinde* with a tradition reaching back through the centuries. It was a corporation chartered by state law; in Germany, any person of Jewish parentage automatically belonged to a Jewish community, from which he could secede only by the act of baptism. These *Gemeinden* were designated to cater for all religious and ritual needs and to render assistance to the sick and the poor. For that reason, they were endowed with authority to tax all Jewish residents. No such institution was to be found in most American villages and towns. Whereas a German-Jewish peddler normally encountered little difficulty in adhering to religious law (kosher food being provided in many places), a peddler in the Alabama backwoods like Henry Lehman was largely left to himself. "Thousands of peddlers wander about America," an observer remarked in 1843. "They no longer put on the phylacteries, they pray neither on working day nor on the Sabbath. In truth they have given up their religion for the pack which is on their backs."[31]

When Henry Lehman settled down in Montgomery, about a dozen Jewish men, some of them with families, lived in the city. They held religious services in the house of a Jewish businessman. At the same house, the first circumcision was performed. Henry joined the circle, which had already been discussing a regular organization of the city's Jews.[32] As elsewhere, an *ad hoc* voluntary association for charitable purposes preceded the founding of a congregation.[33] On November 17, 1846, a society under the name of "Chefra Mefacker Cholim" (society for relieving the sick) was formed, its objects being "a close union of the members of the ancient faith," the "proper observance of our religion," and the provision of "nurses and support for the sick and distressed." Apparently, all twelve founding members (among them Henry Lehman) were of German origin. The society bought a piece of land which was to be used as a Jewish cemetery and organized services in public halls on New Year's Day and the Day of Atonement. Jewish citizens of Selma, Marion, Camden, Tuskegee, Hayneville, and other Alabama towns came to Montgomery and participated.[34] The services on the High Holidays also attracted non-Jews.[35]

As more and more Jews settled in Montgomery, it was unanimously decided at a meeting on May 6, 1849, to organize a congregation. A committee drew up a constitution and bylaws, which were adopted on June 3, 1849. Among the officers of "Kahl Montgomery" elected for one year were twenty-six-year-old Henry Lehman as vice president and Emanuel Lehman, four years his junior, as secretary. The congregation, the third to be established in Alabama, then comprised about thirty members.[36] In most of the new Jewish congregations, services, at first, were conducted in the traditional way. Sermons were often preached and minutes recorded in German.[37] Most certainly this also happened in Montgomery.

[1] *Auswanderung Bremen-USA* (Führer des Deutschen Schiffahrtsmuseums No. 4), Bremerhaven, 1976, pp. 63-64.

[2] Friedrich Gerstäcker, "Reise von Leipzig nach New York. Brieftagebuch einer Überfahrt im Zwischendeck 1837," in *Auf Auswandererseglern. Berichte von Zwischendecks- und Kajütpassagieren* (Führer des Deutschen Schiffahrtsmuseums No. 5), Bremerhaven, 1976, p. 42.

[3] Udo Sauter, *Geschichte der Vereinigten Staaten von Amerika*, Stuttgart, 1976, p. 551.

[4] Weymouth T. Jordan, *Ante-Bellum Alabama. Town and Country. With an Introduction by Kenneth R. Johnson*, Tallahassee, Fla., 1957, reprinted 1987, p. 7.

[5] Nevins, p. 5.

[6] Jordan, p. 174.

[7] Würzburg State Archives, Statistische Sammlung 280; Toury, *Manual Labour*, p. 51.

[8] Jordan, pp. 9, 15.

[9] Jordan, p. 11. According to Jordan, p. 18, in the 1850-1851 season ships from Mobile were transporting cargoes to Great Britain and France, as well as Amsterdam, Rotterdam, Antwerp, Hamburg, Bremen, St. Petersburg, Stockholm, Ghent, Gibraltar, Barcelona, Havana, Genoa, and Trieste.

[10] The National Archives of the United States, National Archives Microfilm Publications, microcopy no. 237, roll 56.

[11] The Würzburg State Archives harbors Jewish marriage, birth, and death certificates from Rimpar, Heidingsfeld, and Rieneck, but not from Heßdorf.

[12] The notarial records in New Orleans contain a will written by Lewis Goldsmith in 1851 in which he states that he is a native of "Hestorf" in Bavaria, born about 1811, and that he had been in America since 1837; Elliott Ashkenazi, Washington, D.C. (letter to the author, April 20, 1995).

[13] Elliott Ashkenazi, *The Business of Jews in Louisiana, 1840-1875*, Tuscaloosa, 1988, p. 109.

[14] Jordan, p. 17.

[15] Ashkenazi, *Business,* pp. 133-135.

[16] Oscar Salomon Straus, *Under Four Administrations.. From Cleveland to Taft,* Boston, New York, 1922, p. 6.

[17] *Centennial*, pp. 1-3; Birmingham, pp. 46-47.

[18] *Centennial*, p. 3; Birmingham, p. 47.

[19] Rudolf Glanz, "The German-Jewish Mass Emigration 1820-1880," in *American Jewish Archives*, vol. 22, April 1970, p. 52.

[20] Harris, pp. 54-55.

[21] Wellhausen, p. 91.

[22] Walker, pp. 79-80. Emanuel's port of disembarkation is unknown.

[23] *Centennial*, p. 3; Nevins, p. 5.

[24] State of Alabama Department of Archives and History, Montgomery, *Montgomery County Marriages*, Book 2A, p. 10.

[25] Harriet later married a man named Moses Weil; Meyer became a junior partner in Lehman Brothers in 1880. Rosenheim and Lehman family tree.

[26] Birmingham, pp. 52, 244.

[27] Avraham Barkai, "German-Jewish Migrations in the Nineteenth Century, 1830-1910," in *Year Book of the Leo Baeck Institute*, vol. 30, 1985, p. 305; Glanz, *Immigration*, p. 82.

[28] Charles Reagan Wilson, William Ferris (eds.), *Encyclopedia of Southern Culture*, Chapel Hill, London, p. 435; Leopold Young, *A Sketch of the First Jewish Settlers of Montgomery, and a Short History of Kahl Montgomery* (typewritten manuscript), Montgomery, 1900, p. 1, made available by the State of Alabama Department of Archives and History, Montgomery.

[29] Ashkenazi, *Business,* p. 9. Even in 1860, there were only 2,000 Jews in Alabama; ibid.

[30] Herbert Philippsthal, "Die Juden in Bayern. Eine statistische Untersuchung," in *Bayerische Israelitische Gemeindezeitung*, No. 5, March 15, 1928, p. 68.

[31] Reissner, p. 84.

[32] Young, p. 1.

[33] Reissner, p. 85.

[34] Young, pp. 1-2; Henry S. Marks, *Past Jewish Life in Alabama* (unpublished manuscript).

[35] Young, p. 2.

[36] Young, p. 2; Marks (unpublished manuscript). The first Jewish community in Alabama had been organized in Mobile in the year 1844; Korn, p. 109.

[37] Reissner, pp. 86, 92-93.

Chapter Six

Revolution

The middle of the nineteenth century saw a heroic effort all over Europe to achieve constitutional government. In the German states, liberals fought for unification and democracy during the abortive revolution of the years 1848 and 1849. Among the objectives of the revolution were full civil rights for German Jews. Initial successes in Berlin, Vienna, and southwest Germany encouraged liberals in their hopes. A German National Assembly convened in Frankfurt. But in 1849, the revolt ended with the triumph of the old powers and was followed by a period of restoration. Active participants were persecuted, and some 4,000 of them eventually went to America.[1]

For a short time, the revolution seemed to be the signal for the final breakthrough into legal and political assimilation for German Jews. Within a few weeks, most German states, among them Bavaria, possessed freedom of the press, the right to found political clubs, and parliaments based on a vastly expanded suffrage. New constitutions were prepared that included religious freedom and emancipation of the Jews. Jews ceased to be excluded from political life; for the first time, they became members of the lower house of the Bavarian Parliament.[2]

According to *The Universal Jewish Encyclopedia*, Maier Lehmann, together with numerous other Jews, played an active part in the revolution. The *Encyclopedia* speaks of his adherence to a group of liberals of which Carl Schurz was another member, and which later made his emigration to the United States desirable.[3] Though this story may sound improbable, it should not be dismissed outright. It is a proven fact that Maier was the intimate friend of another revolutionary, Lazarus Straus from Otterberg in Rhenish Bavaria. Also, in later life, he spoke critically of Germany's undemocratic society.

Maier Lehmann was eighteen in 1848, one year younger than Carl Schurz. While a student in Bonn, Schurz, a non-Jew, joined the revolutionary movement and participated in rebellions in the Rhineland, the Palatinate, and in Baden. After the revolutionaries' final defeat, he escaped to Switzerland, and later to Paris and London. From there Schurz shipped out to New York in the fall of 1852. In America, he was a dedicated supporter of the Republican party and President Abraham Lincoln. He became a senator and was secretary of the Interior under President Rutherford B. Hayes from 1877 to 1881.[4]

Lazarus Straus from Otterberg had been active only locally in the revolutionary movement and was not prosecuted. "He was made aware, however, of the suspicions of the authorities and was subjected to all those petty annoyances and discriminations which a reactionary government never fails to lay upon people who have revolted, and revolted in vain," Lazarus's son Oscar wrote in his memoirs.[5] Like Carl Schurz, Lazarus Straus went to the United States in 1852; his wife and four children followed in 1854. According to Herbert H. Lehman, Oscar Straus, later the first Jewish member of an American cabinet, was "a very intimate friend" of Maier Lehmann: "The families had been friends for several generations." Maier's son Irving married a daughter of Oscar's brother Nathan.[6]

On December 14, 1849, the lower house of the Bavarian parliament passed a bill for Jewish emancipation that mandated complete equality between Jews and Christians. One of the most outspoken opponents of the bill was Dr. Anton Ruland from Lower Franconia. In the debate, he asserted that Jews were still foreigners, even if they had been living in Bavaria for a thousand years.[7] According to Ruland, a Catholic priest who later became librarian of Würzburg's university library, the characters of the Bavarian and the Jewish people were utterly irreconcilable.[8]

Essentially, the law repealed the Jewish Edict that had restricted Jewish life so severely for so long. King Maximilian II's ministers even went much further than Parliament had asked of them in 1846. No other German state initiated such far-reaching legislation on Jews. The result was euphoria among Jews and bitterness among many Christians. A broad movement against emancipation sprang up almost overnight and sent hundreds of petitions to the upper house (*Kammer der Reichsräte*), which had yet to confirm the bill. In Heidingsfeld, the city council submitted a petition draft to the citizens. Led by the mayor and all the councilors, 267 citizens signed it at town hall on a Sunday afternoon. In opposing full emancipation, the citizens of Heidingsfeld cited the presence of a large number of resident Jews as evidence of their knowledge of Jewish life and actions.[9] The campaign culminated in a debate and vote for rejection in the upper house in February 1850. Jewish equality was out of the question, opponents of the bill repeated over and over again, because it would mean that Bavaria would no longer be a Christian state. As a consequence of the government's defeat it took another eleven years until the hated *Matrikelparagraph* was finally abolished.

Maier Lehmann, to be sure, did not want to wait that long, although, with two of his brothers already gone, he probably would not have stayed behind even if the law had been passed. In Würzburg, the *Neue Fränkische Zeitung* published a bitter article on February 28, 1850, in which a Jew advised other Bavarian Jews to seek self-emancipation through emigration.[10] Herbert H. Lehman remembered that his father had strong political reasons for leaving Germany: "(He) felt that it was a completely undemocratic country, and he never got over this distrust of Germany and of the German ruling classes."[11]

When Maier decided to go, he had already met Babette Neugaß, the girl he was to marry in New Orleans several years later, and her sisters. The occasion was his brother Seligmann's marriage on November 2, 1848, to Mathilde Goldschmidt of Heßdorf, the twenty-four-year-old daughter of a cattle dealer named Jakob Goldschmidt. Seligmann was a farmer, the owner of fifteen acres of land.[12]

Mathilde Goldschmidt had an elder sister, Friederike, who, in 1836, had married Isaak Neugaß, a weaver of neighboring Rieneck.[13] On March 15, 1837, Babette, the first child of Isaak and Friederike, was born. Babette had one brother and six sisters: Benjamin (born in 1839), who was to enter into close business contact with the firm, Lehman Brothers, Helena (Hannchen, 1841), Therese (1843), Betti (1845), Fanny (1847; she died in 1848 of apoplexy), Esther (1849), and Klara (1851).[14] "I assume the families knew each other," Maier's son Herbert remarked in 1957 when he was interviewed by the Oral History Research Office of Columbia University. "I

The former Rimpar synagogue is used today as a warehouse (Christian Will, Estenfeld)

think my father knew her as a very little girl," he said of Babette Neugaß.[15] Babette was eleven years old, Maier was twenty, when they met during Seligmann's and Mathilde's marriage.

Some time in May 1850, Maier boarded the ship *Admiral* in Hamburg. On July 17th, he reached New York harbor[16] where he changed his first name to Mayer and, like his brothers, dropped the second "n" in Lehmann. This seemed only natural as the German word "Mann" is "man" in English. In 1850, 1,868 Christians and Jews emigrated from Lower Franconia to the United States. By that year, approximately 50,000 Jews were living in the United States, still slightly fewer than in Bavaria. As soon as Mayer reached Montgomery, *H. Lehman & Bro* became *Lehman Brothers* and Mayer started a two-year apprenticeship as a clerk.[17]

Despite the crushing defeat of the emancipation law in 1850, the Bavarian government immediately began to prepare new legislation designed to provide relief from the most obvious restrictions of the Jewish Edict. In 1851, a law abolished all remaining differences between Jews and Christians in civil law, as far as marriage, property rights, and inheritance were concerned.[18] This, however, was not enough to stop Jewish emigration. A petition, put together in 1855 by Mendel Rosenbaum of Zell near Würzburg, estimated the number of Jewish emigrants from Bavaria between 1830 and 1855 at more than 10,000. Emigration was mainly responsible for the decrease of the Jewish population. Between 1818 and 1871, the number of Jews in Bavaria fell from 53,000 to 50,000, while it almost doubled in Germany as a whole (from 270,000 to 512,000).[19]

It is interesting to note that the Jewish population of Rimpar, contrary to the common trend in rural communities, continued to rise until it reached a peak of 142 men, women, and children in 1867. Because of this atypical development, the Rimpar synagogue had to be enlarged in 1852; a stairway was added that led to the new women's gallery on the upper floor. Also, the interior was refurbished, using elaborate woodwork. The walls were newly painted; some of the colorful ornaments can still be seen today.[20]

[1] Wust, Moos (eds.), p. 42.

[2] Harris, pp. 37-38.

[3] Isaak Landman (ed.), *The Universal Jewish Encyclopedia in ten volumes*, vol. 6, New York, 1942, p. 596.

[4] Wust, Moos (eds.), p. 140.

[5] Straus, *Four Administrations*, pp. 4-5.

[6] Herbert H. Lehman, *Reminiscences,* pp. 15-16.

[7] Harris, p. 70.

[8] Karl-Thomas Remlein, "Der Bayerische Landtag und die Judenemanzipation nach der Revolution 1848," in Brandt (ed.), *Schutzherrschaft*, p. 163.

[9] Harris, pp. 1-2, 172-180; Würzburg State Archives, Regierung von Unterfranken, Präsidialakten 325.

[10] Harris, p. 196.

[11] Herbert H. Lehman, *Reminiscences,* p. 124.

[12] Abraham Lehmann owned less than one acre at the time; Gemeindearchiv Rimpar, Rechnungen I/74b; Würzburg State Archives, Landratsamt Gemünden 260 II.

[13] Würzburg State Archives, Jüdische Standesregister 110. Isaak Neugaß had been matriculated in Rieneck on September 23, 1835; Würzburg State Archives, Statistische Sammlung 617.

[14] Würzburg State Archives, Jüdische Standesregister 110; Würzburg City Archives, Einwohnermeldeamt, Meldebogen Isaak Neugaß. Klara's twin brother was still-born.

[15] Herbert H. Lehman, *Reminiscences,* p. 3.

[16] National Archives Microfilm Publications, Microcopy No. 237, *Passenger Lists of Vessels Arriving at New York 1820-1897,* roll 90, Washington, 1957.

[17] Wellhausen, p. 91; Ashkenazi, *Business,* p. 9; *Centennial,* p. 4.

[18] Harris, p. 197.

[19] Gehring-Münzel, *Schutzjude,* p. 194.

[20] Will, Siegler, pp. 179-183.

Chapter Seven

The House of Lehman

"They had a little store," Herbert Lehman said about the origins of Lehman Brothers in antebellum Montgomery. "It developed quite rapidly into a general store. Their main business was buying cotton. It was used as currency in the South in those days. It was largely a barter arrangement. The farmers would come in with their cotton and trade it for shirts and shoes and fertilizer, such little fertilizer as was used in those days, and seed, and all the necessities. That's how they got started in the cotton business."[1]

Home of the Mayer Lehman family in Montgomery, Alabama (Herbert H. Lehman Suite and Papers, Columbia University, New York.)

"Cotton is king!" was a slogan often heard in Montgomery in those years. Water- and steam-driven spinning mills multiplied in New England and in Great Britain, creating an enormous demand for cotton. Montgomery became a center for the storage of cotton before it was sold to Mobile and New Orleans for shipment to New York. It was a boom town in a boom time. America's frontiers were pushed forward; roads, railroads, and factories were built at an incredible rate. The goods

55

Lehman Brothers had to offer were in great demand, as was cotton, accepted as payment. Two years after Mayer's arrival, the transactions of the firm started to appear regularly in the records of the *County Clerk*. The city directory listed the brothers as "grocers," a designation far more comprehensive than its present-day usage; it embraced wholesalers of commodities and consumer goods of all types. The Lehmans extended long-range credits in trading with planters who had no income until their crop was ready for sale in the fall, and settled accounts in bales of cotton more often than in dollars. This was typical of general storekeepers located in cotton-growing areas. Once in a while, they also bought a little cotton outright. In the course of time, the brothers increased their cotton purchases.[2]

It did not take long until the Lehmans had actually become dealers in cotton, merely keeping their general store as an adjunct. Emanuel made annual trips to New York to replenish their shelves and negotiate with cotton manufacturers and exporters. For the cotton sold, the firm received drafts on New York banks or bills on London, which Emanuel exchanged for cash in New York. Henry, in turn, went to New Orleans, the major receiving point for the cotton crop, while Mayer managed the store and kept in close touch with planters and farmers.[3]

New Orleans had long attracted German immigrants, among them many Jews. As early as 1842, a German-language newspaper *(Der Deutsche Courier)* was founded. New Orleans Jews, numerous enough to organize three synagogues, were an active force in commerce, finance, music, and journalism.[4] While on one of his business trips to New Orleans, Henry Lehman became ill with yellow fever in the current epidemic. He died on November 17, 1855, at the age of thirty-three, leaving a widow and four small children.[5] Henry was buried in New Orleans. His brothers, Emanuel, twenty-eight years old and of conservative temper, and Mayer, twenty-five and more buoyant and sociable, were left to carry on. According to historian Elliott Ashkenazi, the two remaining Lehmans dealt with ever-growing quantities of cotton: "To increase their purchasing power beyond the advances received from those who bought cotton from them, the Lehmans established an informal banking operation in Montgomery based on loans to cotton growers secured by crop liens. The source of the loans was deposits left with Lehman Brothers. These were secured by warehouse receipts covering cotton in their own warehouses. The amount of money involved in the cotton transactions justified the opening of an office in New York in 1858 to faciliate the handling of the financial aspects of the cotton trade. Emanuel Lehman moved to New York to manage the new office."[6]

The first New York office of Lehman Brothers was established at 119 Liberty Street, with Emanuel living in Manhattan. Mayer, the man with expert knowledge of cotton, remained in Alabama. On May 22, 1859, Emanuel married Pauline Sondheim, daughter of Louis Sondheim of New York. The couple had five children: Milton, Philip, Evelyn, Harriet, and Albert.[7]

After Henry's death, Mayer had taken over many of his late brother's responsibilities, including regular trips to New Orleans. In that city he frequented the house of the Goldsmith (formerly Goldschmidt) family, whose roots, as mentioned above, also went back to Lower Franconia. The Goldsmiths, after leaving Mobile, now ran a successful wholesale dry goods business. It was in their residence that Mayer Lehman came across Babette Neugaß (Newgass, by then[8]), who had come to New Orleans from Rieneck some time after 1854.[9] Babette, her sisters Esther and Betti, and her brother Benjamin were part of an immense new wave of emigration from Germany. Between 1850 and 1859, almost one million Germans arrived in the United States.[10] Mayer's and Babette's marriage was performed in New Orleans on January 6, 1858, three days before Mayer's twenty-eighth birthday. The bride, a vivacious and strong-minded young woman, was twenty. Among the witnesses was Abraham Haber, partner in Lewis Goldsmith's business.[11]

The first synagogue of Montgomery on Catoma Street and Church Street (State of Alabama Department of Archives and History, Montgomery)

After their return to Montgomery, Mayer and Babette, in the words of their son Herbert, "entered into the social life very well." They "became relatively prosperous" within a short time and "had a surprisingly nice house," a very substantial-looking building, big enough for Mayer's clerks to come over and have their meals there.[12] The four eldest children were born in the Montgomery house: Sigmund (1859), Hattie (Harriet, 1861), Settie (Lisette, 1863), and Benjamin (1865), who died in infancy.[13]

By the time the Civil War broke out, Mayer's family had very definitely established itself. The city had grown during recent years and now counted a population of 9,000. Massive brick mansions and the capitol on Goat Hill with its glistening white dome had been erected. Babette and Mayer enjoyed Montgomery life in the last years before the war; the Lehmans had become part of the political, social, and economic structure of the South. Mayer, a staunch Democrat, associated with the state's leading politicians, and the couple was invited to the houses of other sucessful businessmen.[14] When he became a member of Montgomery's Masonic lodge, Mayer Lehman gained the definite seal of civic approval.[15]

After his brother Henry had died and Emanuel had moved to New York, Mayer continued the family's work for the young Jewish congregation. He acted as treasurer for the period 1859 to 1861 and as trustee from 1862 to 1863. In April 1859, a committee on building a synagogue was appointed, with Mayer Lehman as one of its five members. Two months later, the committee bought a corner plot on Catoma Street and Church Street. Three years later, on March 8, 1862, the new synagogue was opened. The dedication services were conducted by Rabbi James K. Gutheim of New Orleans, who was to become minister[16] of the congregation one year later. During the ceremony, as Leopold Young reports, "the first innovation from established customs took place; a choir with music participated in the services." During the same year, a Jewish school was organized where not only religious but also secular branches were taught. Shortly afterward, the congregation elected an official who served as cantor, ritual slaughterer, and teacher.[17] Only then had Jewish life in Montgomery reached the institutional level to which the Lehman brothers had been accustomed in Rimpar.

[1] Lehman, *Reminiscences,* p. 2.

[2] *Centennial,* pp. 3-4; Ashkenazi, *Business,* p. 127.

[3] Nevins, pp. 5-7; Ashkenazi, *Business,* p. 127.

[4] Ashkenazi, *Business,* p. 9; Nevins, p. 4; Henry Marx, "Michael Hahn (1830-1886), Gouverneur von Louisiana," in Manfred Treml, Wolf Weigand (eds.), *Geschichte und Kultur der Juden in Bayern. Lebensläufe* (Veröffentlichungen zur Bayerischen Geschichte und Kultur, No. 18/88), München, 1988, p. 153.

[5] *Centennial,* p. 6. The date 1855 is also given by the Rosenheim and Lehman family tree. According to Nevins, p. 7, Henry Lehman died in 1856.

[6] Ashkenazi, *Business,* pp. 127-128.

[7] Marks (unpublished manuscript); Rosenheim and Lehman family tree. Of the children, only Philip rose to prominence. He became a partner in Lehman Brothers in 1885. It was at his insistence that the firm first began to venture into underwriting, the step that eventually led Lehman Brothers into investment banking. Philip's son Robert became head of the firm in 1925 and put together one of the most famous art collections in the United States. Birmingham, pp. 332, 379-380.

[8] The meaning of the German name "Neugaß" is "new lane." "ß" is a German letter used instead of "ss."

[9] Ashkenazi, *Business,* p. 109; Central Archives for the History of the Jewish People, Jerusalem, WR 15.

[10] Wust, Moos (eds.), p. 46.

[11] A copy of the marriage certificate was made available by the Herbert H. Lehman Suite and Papers at Columbia University, New York.

[12] Lehman, *Reminiscences,* pp. 3-4.

[13] Sigmund was made a partner in Lehman Brothers in 1882. He married his first cousin, Emanuel's daughter Harriet. Their grandchild Orin Lehman was born in 1922. He became a captain in the U.S. Army in World War II. Seriously wounded, losing most of his face and almost both of his legs, he was awarded the Purple Heart and the Distinguished Flying Cross. He went on to become an important figure in New York State, holding many positions, including most recently, commissioner of parks for the State of New York. Orin Lehman was also the founder and first chairman of Just One Break, a major charity to help disabled people. Hattie Lehman married Philip J. Goodhart. In his book, *Our Crowd*, Stephen Birmingham paints a loving picture of her (pp. 3-8). The Goodharts' son Arthur was a professor of jurisprudence and the first American master of an Oxford University College; his son Sir Philip Goodhart became a member of the British Parliament. Philip and Hattie Goodhart's daughter Helen married Frank Altschul of Lazard Frères; the Altschuls' son Arthur became a partner of Goldman, Sachs, a civic leader, and art collector. In 1992, he visited Rimpar and held talks with Mayor Anton Kütt and Christian Will, then a member of the Bavarian Parliament. Settie Lehman married Morris Fatman, a manufacturer of cloth; their daughter, Elinor, became the wife of Henry Morgenthau, Jr., who, from 1934 to 1945, was secretary of the treasury under President Franklin D. Roosevelt. The Morgenthaus' son Robert is the longtime district attorney for New York County. Rosenheim and Lehman family tree; John L. Loeb, Jr. (letter to the author, November 1, 1995); Lehman Family Reunion Press Release, June 1989, made available by John L. Loeb, Jr.; Nevins, p. 35; Morgenthau, passim.

[14] Nevins, pp. 8-9.

[15] On November 5, 1860, Mayer Lehman supported the petition for membership of a Montgomery bookkeeper; Masonic Collection, State of Alabama Department of Archives and History, Montgomery.

[16] Many Jewish congregations in America had a professional leader, usually an ordained rabbi who had received his training in Europe. A majority of the rabbis of the 1800s were also called ministers; Henry Marks, Marsha Kass Marks, "Jewish Life in Alabama: The Formative Stages," in *Alabama Heritage*, vol. 36 (Spring 1995), p. 8.

[17] Young, pp. 3-6.

Chapter Eight

Civil War

Eighteen-sixty-two was a year that would be remembered for other events: in April, one year after the first shot of the Civil War was fired at Fort Sumter, Union troops took New Orleans. In August, General Robert E. Lee's Confederate army was victorious at Bull Run. On September 22, President Abraham Lincoln declared all slaves living in the Confederate States of America to be free as of January 1, 1863.[1]

Montgomery was the cradle of the secession. Its cannons roared and its bells rang out when delegates of six seceding states met there on February 4, 1861. On February 11, Jefferson Davis of Mississippi was elected president, and a week later he accepted the wild acclaim of throngs in Court Square, near the office of Lehman Brothers. Until the government moved to Richmond four months later, Montgomery was the capital of the Confederacy.[2]

The outbreak of the Civil War in April 1861 was a staggering blow to Lehman Brothers. The New York office, cut off from its southern supply of cotton, was practically closed down and the Montgomery branch, cut off from northern manufacturers, was put on a limited basis. *"Alles ist beendet!"* ("All is finished!") Emanuel scrawled despairingly on a pad in his office.[3] Both brothers, like most Southern Jews, identified strongly with the Confederate cause. "Jews in the South accepted the southern cause despite their recent arrival in the region. They supported the Confederacy because they lived there," Elliott Ashkenazi has said.[4] Not only did Jews fight in the Confederate regiments,[5] they assumed positions within the military and political leadership, including the offices of surgeon general, judge advocate, quartermaster general, and secretary of state.[6] Jews such as Rabbi Maximilian Michelbacher of Richmond could be counted among the defenders of all Southern institutions, including slavery.[7]

The Lehman brothers, who had not enjoyed personal freedom at home and had left Bavaria for that very reason, were now living in a country where a considerable part of the population was held as slaves. Like most other Southern Jews, they did not openly question the institution of slavery, which "was an axiomatic foundation of the social pattern of the Old South. Jews wanted to acclimate themselves in every way to their environment; in both a social and psychological sense, they needed to be accepted as equals by their fellow-citizens," as historian Bertram Wallace Korn has observed.[8] Lazarus Straus, Mayer Lehman's friend from Bavaria, had become a storekeeper in Talbotton, Georgia. According to his son Oscar, "the grown people of the South, whatever they thought about (slavery), would not, except in rare instances, speak against it; and even then in the most private and guarded manner. To do otherwise would subject one to social ostracism." Hired slaves who worked for the Straus family would beg to be bought by them. "As a result of such pleadings,"

Jefferson Davis, president of the Confederacy, is sworn in on the balcony of the State House in Montgomery on February 18, 1861 (National Archives, Washington D.C.)

Oscar wrote, "my father purchased household slaves one by one from their masters, although neither he nor my mother believed in slavery."[9] There may have been others who owned slaves for similar reasons. There may also have been merchants who took a slave as security for a debt.

Montgomery county with its huge plantations was one of the counties in which slave population was densest, with an average of ten slaves to the household in 1860.[10] In that year, Mayer Lehman owned seven slaves, four women and three men.[11] Some of these were household slaves, others may have been used in the firm. Household slaves were often regarded as members of the family,[12] and it comes as no surprise that at least two former slaves followed the Lehmans to New York after the war. One, a woman, brought up several of Mayer's and Babette's children.[13]

Offices of Lehman, Durr & Co on Court Square, Montgomery, shortly after the Civil War (Herbert H. Lehman Suite and Papers, Columbia University, New York)

After President Abraham Lincoln imposed a blockade on the Confederacy, Lehman Brothers were cut off from their New York outpost and unable to import manufactured goods from the North. Logically, they turned even more intensively to cotton. The war never completely stopped cotton trading. The Confederacy hoped cotton would pay for its military needs and provide security to attract European loans. The Union, on the other hand, needed cotton for its war effort. Small cotton shipments could be sneaked through the blockade or sent to New York via England.[14]

The remaining cotton, however, had to be stored until the war was over. To strengthen its operation in cotton, Mayer cooperated with a Montgomery cotton merchant named John Wesley Durr. In 1863, Lehman and Durr, co-owner of the Alabama Warehouse, one of Montgomery's principal cotton centers, formed a partnership under the name of Lehman, Durr and Company and bought the warehouse.[15]

After New Orleans was occupied by a Union fleet in April 1862, Mayer moved some of his operations to that city, where a brother of his wife, twenty-three-year-old Benjamin Newgass, was living. Benjamin had been in the tobacco business in Louisville, Kentucky. Before the end of the war, an office was established under the name of Lehman, Newgass & Co. It functioned in much the same way as Lehman Brothers in antebellum Montgomery, selling general merchandise wholesale and, at the same time, concentrating on the cotton market.[16] According to Elliott Ashkenazi, business connections among family members and in-laws were frequent among Jews in the South: "Lines between the personal and business affairs of these Jews were always vague; the trust generated by family ties was a valuable asset in a business arrangement."[17]

For a time, Emanuel Lehman went to England where he was employed by the Confederate government in efforts to sell its bonds. When these efforts failed, he returned to New York.[18] In the fall of 1863, Emanuel decided to travel to Europe again. With him were his wife, Pauline, and three children. On December 12, 1863, the family arrived in Würzburg, where it was going to spend some weeks.[19] Certainly Emanuel presented his family to his brother Seligmann, whose wife had just had a baby.

Emanuel's and Seligmann's mother, Eva Lehmann, had died of consumption ten years earlier, on July 19, 1853. Like her children Fratel, Samuel, and Moses, who died in infancy, she was buried in the Jewish cemetery of Schwanfeld.[20] Almost one and a half centuries later, the gravestone still stands erect in the oldest part of the cemetery. The epigraph is in Hebrew; on the back of the stone, "E. Lehmann" is written in Latin letters.

One year after the death of his mother, Seligmann moved to Heidingsfeld with his wife Mathilde and their daughters, Gela and Hanna. In 1856, he was listed as a cattle dealer. Within the next years, six more children were born: Eva, obviously named after his mother (1856), Lisette (1858), a child whose name is illegible (1859), Jakob (1861), Benzion (1863), and Adolph (1866).[21] Seligmann's widowed father, Abraham Lehmann, was sixty-nine in 1854 and probably no longer active in his profession. So it seems only natural that he should have gone to Heidingsfeld with his son, where he certainly moved into the latter's house.

One year after the family get-together in Heidingsfeld, the American Civil War was drawing to its close. An episode in the final months of the Confederacy throws some light on Mayer Lehman's role as a prominent Southern citizen. Concerned with the plight of Confederate soldiers in prison camps of the Union, the Alabama Legislature authorized Governor Thomas Hill Watts to spend $500,000 for the relief of Alabama captives. For the money, cotton was to be purchased and then, with the Union's consent, shipped through Mobile or New Orleans to the North and sold. The proceeds were to be used by an agent of the state to supply the prisoners with clothing, blankets, and medicines. The governor trusted his friend Mayer Lehman with the task. On December 14, 1864, Watts wrote the following letter to President Jefferson Davis: "I have appointed Mr. Mayer Lehman as the agent of the State, under this act, with instructions to proceed immediately to Richmond to have, if possible, the contemplated arrangement made. I have furnished him with instructions. He will call on you and present this letter. He is a businessman of established character and one of the best Southern patriots. He is a foreigner, but has been here fifteen years and is thoroughly identified with us. It will be necessary for him to get through the lines. I ask that he may be furnished with proper passports and endorsed by you as the Agent of the State of Alabama, to comply with the act of the Legislature to visit the Northern prisons, and to provide for the Alabama soldiers there in prison."[22]

Eva Lehmann's grave (center back) in the Jewish cemetery of Schwanfeld (Roland Flade, Würzburg)

Governor Watts added that the Reverend Isaac Taylor Tichenor would accompany Mayer as assistant. Lehman and Tichenor immediately went to Richmond. On January 14, 1865, after a meeting with President Davis, they wrote a letter to the commander of the Union forces, General Ulysses S. Grant: "General: We have the honor to announce to you that the State of Alabama has appropriated $500,000 for the relief of prisoners from that State held by your Government. The undersigned having been appointed agents for the purpose of carrying into effect the design of this appropriation, most respectfully ask, through you, permission to proceed to the United States on the object of our mission. Having obtained permission from the Confederate Government to ship cotton to the amount of this appropriation, we are instructed by the Governor of Alabama to ask permission to pass it through the blockade. We would further state that it would be agreeable to the Governor of Alabama if a vessel of the United States should be permitted to carry this cotton to the port of New York, to be there sold and the proceeds applied to the purchase of blankets, clothing, and such other things as may be needed for the comfort of prisoners from that State. We beg leave to suggest Mobile Bay as the point from which this cotton may be shipped. We deem it proper to state that our mission is confined strictly to the object stated. It embraces nothing of a military or political nature, and if permitted to carry out the design of our State we will cheerfully submit to such rules, regulations, and paroles as are usual in such cases. We well know that a gallant soldier must feel for those brave men who by the fortunes of war are held as prisoners, exposed to the rigors of a climate to which they are not accustomed, the severities of which are augmented by the privations necessarily attendant upon their condition. We ask this favor with confidence, assured that your sympathies for the unfortunate brave will lead you to do all in your power to promote the benevolent design entrusted to us by the State of Alabama.

We have the honor to be, most respectfully, your obedient servants, M. Lehman. I. T. Tichenor, Agents for the State of Alabama."[23]

Receiving no answer, Mayer and his lieutenant on the relief mission again wrote to Grant, adding a copy of the original letter. The permission, however, never came. General Grant refused to pass Mayer Lehman through the lines. The Washington government had decided upon tactics of relentless attrition to end the war quickly. After having waited in Richmond through a cold January, Mayer Lehman and the Reverend Tichenor returned to Montgomery. On April 9, 1865, Robert E. Lee surrendered to Grant at Appomattox Court House.[24] A few days later, John W. Booth, a former actor and Southern extremist, shot President Abraham Lincoln.

To keep it out of Union hands, retreating Confederate troops set fire to the cotton stored in the Alabama Warehouse before they left Montgomery.[25] While Mayer Lehman inspected the ruins and made plans for reconstruction, his father's life ended thousands of miles away. Abraham Lehmann surely knew from his son Emanuel about the Civil War. Five days after Lincoln's death, he died in Heidingsfeld on April 20, 1865.[26]

---

[1] Victor Austin (ed.), *Der Amerikanische Bürgerkrieg in Augenzeugenberichten*, München, 1973, pp. 335-336.

[2] *Centennial*, p. 9.

[3] Birmingham, p. 70.

[4] Ashkenazi, *Business*, p. 25.

[5] Approximately 1,200 Jews served in the Confederacy, including thirty-five officers; other ac-

counts have placed the number as high as 10,000; Eli N. Evans, *The Provincials. A Personal History of Jews in the South,* New York, 1973, p. 62.

[6] Wilson, Ferris (eds.), p. 435. After six months as secretary of war, Judah Benjamin became secretary of state of the Confederacy, a post he retained until the surrender of General Lee; Benjamin Kaplan, "Judah Philip Benjamin," in Dinnerstein, Palsson (eds.), *Jews in the South,* pp. 85-87.

[7] Wilson, Ferris (eds.), p. 435.

[8] Korn, p. 96.

[9] Straus, pp. 12-13.

[10] Nevins, p. 6.

[11] Eighth Census (1860), Slave Inhabitants of Alabama; information provided by Henry S. Marks, Huntsville, Alabama.

[12] Straus, p. 13.

[13] Herbert H. Lehman, *Reminiscences*, p. 4.

[14] *Centennial,* p. 9; Ashkenazi, *Business,* p. 24; Birmingham, pp. 76-77.

[15] John Wesley Durr was born in Harris County, Georgia, in 1835. At the age of seventeen, he moved to Montgomery. His partnership with Lehman Brothers continued until 1891, when the firm was incorporated as the Lehman-Durr Company, of which Durr was president. In 1863 and again in 1875, Durr was elected alderman of the city of Montgomery. John Wesley Durr's granddaughter-in-law, Virginia Durr, was a friend of Martin Luther King, Jr., and a leader of the Civil Rights movement in Montgomery. She wrote a book, *Outside the Magic Circle,* about her experience. Her sister married Hugo Black, the famous Supreme Court justice appointed by President Franklin D. Roosevelt. Hilary A. Herbert, *Memorial Record of Alabama, Historical and Biographical,* Montgomery, 1893; Hollinger F. Barnard (ed.), *Outside the Magic Circle. The Autobiography of Virginia Foster Durr,* University, Alabama, 1985.

[16] Ashkenazi, *Business,* p. 128.

[17] Ashkenazi, *Business,* p. 105.

[18] Nevins, p. 9.

[19] Würzburg City Archives, Einwohnermeldeamt, Meldebogen Emanuel Lehman.

[20] Würzburg State Archives, Jüdische Standesregister 111.

[21] Würzburg City Archives, Heidingsfelder Ratsprotokolle 22, pp. 403-404; Würzburg State Archives, Jüdische Standesregister 40, Regierung von Unterfranken 14071.

[22] United States, War Dept., Series II, *The War of the Rebellion*, vol. 7, p. 1223.

[23] *War of the Rebellion,* vol. 8, pp. 69-70.

[24] *Centennial,* p. 12; Austin (ed.), p. 339.

[25] Ashkenazi, *Business,* p. 128. Virgina Durr tells the following story about the partnership of her grandfather-in-law, John Wesley Durr, and the Lehmans: The Lehmans and the Durrs had saved a considerable sum of money which they turned into gold. When Union troops occupied Montgomery, the only safe place for this gold seemed under the skirts of Mrs. John Wesley Durr. Durr and Lehman believed that Union troops, whom they considered uncivilized compared to Confederate troops, would not search under a woman's skirts. After the Union troops had left, the gold was divided between the Lehmans and the Durrs. The Durr family went on to found a successful pharmaceutical company by the name of The Durr Drug Company. It became, in due course, the Durr-Fillauer Medical Company. In 1992, a major American corporation, Bergen Brunswig, bought control of the firm. John L. Loeb, Jr. (letter to the author, September 27, 1995).

[26] Würzburg State Archives, Jüdische Standesregister 41.

Chapter Nine

Liverpool and New York

The Civil War had torn the country apart, and it was a long time until Northern and Southern states were reconciled. Until the seceding states were fully reinstated in the Union, a sort of military government was set up in the South. Corruption and disorder under the so-called "carpetbag regimes" were widespread. Slavery had come to an end without a land reform program to dismantle plantations and distribute the land among the freedmen. As a consequence, many former slaves kept tied to the planters' land through sharecropping arrangements.[1] Northern journalists who visited the postbellum South sent back reports of a devastated society. After three years of fighting, Northern Alabama and the state's central counties, which had felt the wrath of the Union cavalry early in 1865, offered scenes of absolute devastation with houses razed, fields uncultivated, and iron works and cotton gins burnt.[2]

Mayer Lehman in Würzburg in 1867 (Herbert H. Lehman Suite and Papers, Columbia University, New York)

Whereas Mobile had been half-destroyed, Montgomery (apart from the burnt-down warehouses) was spared. With Emanuel resuming the operations of Lehman Brothers in New York, Mayer was ready to reassemble the pieces of Lehman, Durr & Co in Montgomery, focusing the firm's efforts overwhelmingly, as before, on cotton. The state of Alabama desperately needed money. The Lehmans came to the aid of the government and lent it $100,000. As a consequence, the Montgomery branch of Lehman Brothers was appointed fiscal agent of the state in 1867, selling its bonds and servicing Alabama's debts, interest payments, and other obligations.[3] In the same year, Mayer, possibly for the first time since his emigration, paid a visit to the country of his birth. A photograph taken in Würzburg shows a full-bearded, self-assured man of thirty-seven.[4]

One thing Mayer definitely wanted was to get away from racial and political strife in Alabama. He saw that John W. Durr and Benjamin Newgass could manage the Montgomery and New Orleans businesses by themselves. He also saw that the center of gravity of Lehman Brothers was shifting to New York. Thus, Mayer decided to follow his brother Emanuel. The administration of the two southern companies, in which the Lehmans held majority interests, was entrusted to the resident partners. In 1868, Mayer moved to New York. A few months earlier, Lehman Brothers had taken new offices in Pearl Street, just off Hanover Square, the booming center of the cotton trade.[5] "My father had come alone to New York, and my mother and three children (one had died) followed him," Mayer's son Herbert said later. His mother told him "about the hardships of travel in the South immediately after the War, and how difficult it was to bring her family from Alabama to New York. For some time after the War, there was very little communication between the South and Washington. The railroads had been destroyed. She told us that when she got to the Potomac, there was a bridge across, but there was no railroad connection."[6]

In New Orleans, dynamic Benjamin Newgass, local head of Lehman, Newgass & Co, was also thinking about moving. For the time being, he was more than busy, however, and had to put off such plans. In 1866, New Orleans handled nearly a third of all the cotton shipped from American ports, much of it going through Benjamin's hands. In that year, a man named Henry Abraham, a brother-in-law of Lewis Goldsmith's son Ferdinand, contributed $50,000 to Lehman, Newgass & Co as the first step to becoming a partner. The Goldsmith family also invested money with the Lehmans. In 1872, the New Orleans firm owned three warehouses for the storage of cotton.[7]

In the year 1872, Benjamin Newgass finally left New Orleans and sailed to Liverpool, the English cotton center, there to establish his own firm. Henry Abraham replaced him as resident partner, and the New Orleans business took on the new name of Lehman, Abraham & Co. When Henry Abraham also left, matters still stayed within the family. Babette Newgass's sister Betti had emigrated to Liverpool where she married a man named Abraham Stern.[8] His younger brother, Maurice, became the new resident partner. The New Orleans firm changed its name again and was now called Lehman, Stern & Co.[9] By then, Babette's sister Esther had left Bavaria for the United States. She married Isaiah Hellman, founder of the first bank

The Neugass Family and the Lehmans – Sterns – Hellmans

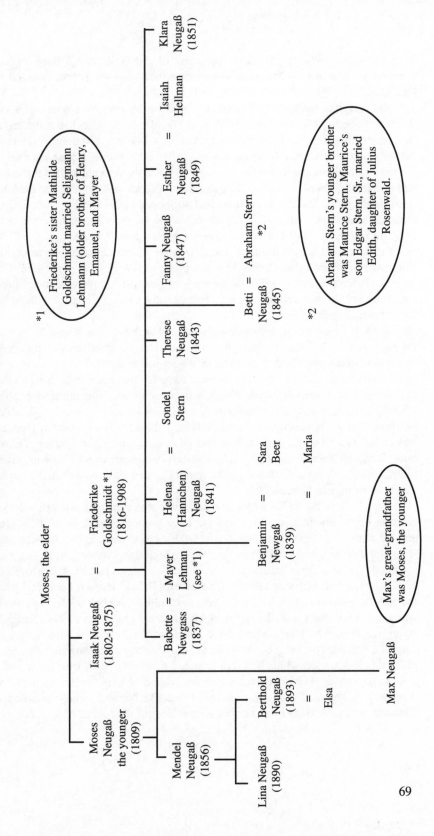

*1 Friederike's sister Mathilde Goldschmidt married Seligmann Lehmann (older brother of Henry, Emanuel, and Mayer

Moses, the elder

Isaak Neugaß (1802–1875) = Friederike Goldschmidt *1 (1816–1908)

Moses Neugaß the younger (1809)

Babette Newgass (1837) = Mayer Lehman (see *1)

Helena (Hannchen) Neugaß (1841) = Sondel Stern

Therese Neugaß (1843)

Betti Neugaß (1845) = Abraham Stern *2

Fanny Neugaß (1847)

Esther Neugaß (1849) = Isaiah Hellman

Klara Neugaß (1851)

Benjamin Newgaß (1839) = Sara Beer

= Maria

*2 Abraham Stern's younger brother was Maurice Stern. Maurice's son Edgar Stern, Sr., married Edith, daughter of Julius Rosenwald.

Mendel Neugaß (1856)

Lina Neugaß (1890)

Berthold Neugaß (1893) = Elsa

Max Neugaß

Max's great-grandfather was Moses, the younger

69

in Los Angeles, who later became president of the Wells Fargo Bank in San Francisco.[10] Babette's other three sisters, together with her parents, stayed in Germany.[11]

In Liverpool, the system of family cooperation became even more elaborate. So far, members of the Lehman, Newgass, and Goldsmith families had commercial ties, connecting New York, Montgomery, and New Orleans, with John W. Durr as the only non-relative and the only non-Jew. After Benjamin Newgass's arrival in Liverpool, the Rosenheim family, the family of Abraham Lehmann's wife, came into the picture. Joseph, one of Leopold Rosenheim's sons, had emigrated to England from Heidingsfeld and, for some time, had been head of the London wine firm L. Rosenheim & Sons. Around 1872, he moved to Liverpool and, together with Benjamin Newgass, founded the cotton house of Newgass, Rosenheim & Co.[12] The new firm acted as Lehman Brothers' agents. The New York Lehmans bought cotton from their Southern offices and sold it at a profit to Newgass, Rosenheim & Co, their English relatives.[13] In 1875, Benjamin Newgass and Joseph Rosenheim split; each founded his own cotton firm and separately the two men continued to act as the Lehmans' agents.[14]

In 1870, an estimated 80,000 Jews lived in New York, almost nine percent of the city's population. The Jewish community was firmly controlled by a network of families in mid-town Manhattan, most of whom had emigrated from Germany a generation earlier. Like the Lehmans, many of these families had accumulated capital in some smaller center, often in the South, had moved to New York during or shortly after the Civil War, and had emerged from retail trade into manufacturing, finance, or wholesale merchandising. The heads of these families, meeting at the synagogue and on the same boards for hospitals and other charitable agencies, felt a close bond. Their children, completely Americanized in contrast to their parents, often intermarried. Mayer's firstborn son, Sigmund, even married his first cousin, Emanuel's daughter Harriet.[15]

New York in the 1870s was a city still without skyscrapers and with a lot of room in upper Manhattan, which was yet largely undeveloped. In 1876, Mayer erected a house at 5 East 62nd Street, a five-floor-brownstone in the characteristic style of the period, very comfortable and with a high stoop, as Herbert H. Lehman recorded.[16] In New York, Babette and Mayer had four more children: Clara (born in 1870), Arthur (1873), Irving (1876), and Herbert (1878).[17] Herbert Lehman, by far the best-known member of the family, went into politics (see below). Irving's name was a substitute for Isaak, the name of his maternal grandfather Isaak Neugaß. Irving Lehman, who later became chief justice of the New York State Court of Appeals, was a deeply religious man; he put together one of the largest collections of Judaica in America, which he left to Temple Emanu-El of the City of New York. It includes a silver Havdalah plate, embossed around 1670 in the Bavarian city of Augsburg. It was used in his grandmother Friederike Neugaß's house to hold the wine cup for the blessing over the wine on the close of the sabbath.[18]

70

*The Mayer Lehman family, about 1886. First row, left to right: Herbert H.
Lehman, Irving Lehman. Second row, seated, left to right: Harriet/Hattie (Mrs.
Philip J. Goodhart) with daughter Helen on lap, Mayer Lehman with grandson
Howard L. Goodhart on lap, Babette Lehman with grandson Allan Lehman on
lap, Lisette/Settie (Mrs. Morris Fatman) with daughter Margaret on lap. Top
row, left to right: Philip J. Goodhart, Harriet (Mrs. Sigmund M. Lehman),
Sigmund M. Lehman, Clara (later Mrs. Richard Limburg), Morris Fatman,
Arthur Lehman. (Herbert H. Lehman Suite and Papers, Columbia University,
New York)*

*Neugaß family Havdalah plate,
given to Irving Lehman by his
grandmother Friederike Neugaß
(Photograph: Will Brown,
Philadelphia. Courtesy of
Congregation Emanu-El of the
City of New York)*

71

Mayer Lehman, in the words of his son Herbert, "was devout and took great pride in his faith and was very, very loyal to it." Mayer spoke and read Hebrew fluently. His wife also observed the religious holidays and went to the synagogue regularly on Saturdays, sometimes on Friday nights. She insisted that her children also observe the Holy Days. Until her old age, Babette refrained from writing on the sabbath. Mayer's and Emanuel's families kept the Day of Atonement, Passover, Hanukkah, and New Year's Day together. Herbert has said, however, that both his father and mother were not particularly affected by ritual or by forms. They had been Orthodox when they came to the United States, but belonged to a congregation slowly on the move toward reform in Montgomery and joined an outright reform synagogue, Temple Emanu-El, in New York.[19]

Interior of Temple Emanu-El in New York, decorated for the 75th anniversary service in April, 1920 (Courtesy of Congregation Emanu-El of the City of New York)

Reform Judaism was the answer of many American Jews to the question how far they wanted to integrate themselves into a basically non-Jewish society. Reform Judaism, as preached by Rabbi Dr. Gustav Gottheil of Temple Emanu-El, omitted all prayers for a return to Palestine, and for the rebuilding of the temple in Jerusalem. In the Pittsburgh Platform, adopted in 1885, it committed itself to the doctrine that Judaism was "a progressive religion, ever striving to be in accord with the postulates of reason." In Temple Emanu-El, women worshipped alongside the men and not in a separate gallery.[20] Until the 1880s, Congregation Emanu-El was composed largely of people who had come over from Germany, or their children, and the service was conducted in German. For many years, Mayer Lehman was a member of the board of trustees of the congregation; he also served on various committees. Later, his son Irving became a trustee and president.[21]

Like his brother, Emanuel, Mayer was a member of the Independent Order of B'nai B'rith, a Jewish organization founded in 1843 with humanitarian and philantropic purposes. Also, like Emanuel, Mayer was active in a number of charitable agencies, not only Jewish ones. The organization that particularly appealed to him was Mount Sinai Hospital. When he withdrew from the administration of Temple Emanu-El, it was to devote more time and labor to the hospital. For nineteen years, he was a member of the board of directors which met on Sunday mornings. Mayer also supported the orphan asylum of the Hebrew Sheltering Guardian Society of New York, the Lebanon Hospital on Westchester Avenue, the Montefiore Home for Chronic Invalids, and the Hebrew Infant Asylum of the City of New York, and he gave money for educational purposes. His wife, Babette, was active in charitable work, too. She was connected with several organizations, but particularly with the Home for Infirm and Aged Hebrews on West 105th Street.[22]

Even decades after Babette's and Mayer's emigration, the family stayed in close contact with their German relatives. Letters and telegrams were exchanged and visits were paid. Mayer had little love for his country of birth, and his antipathy, in a way, was well founded. Quite rightly Mayer recalled Germany "as a country of great castes. Even before Hitler came in there was a great deal of anti-Semitism there and a great deal of social discrimination. It was virtually impossible for a Jew to become a member of the faculty of any of the universities. It was almost impossible for a Jew to join any of the fraternal organizations." (Herbert H. Lehman)[23]

Often, the family visited Lower Franconia where Babette's parents and two of her sisters were still living. In Heidingsfeld, they also met Mayer's and Emanuel's brother, Seligmann, whose children must have been greatly impressed by their American relatives. So impressed were they by the tales of their uncles' rise in the United States that three of them decided to cross the Atlantic as well. Around 1870, Seligmann's second eldest daughter, Hanna, emigrated to Texas at the age of seventeen. In Galveston, she married Jacob Northmann, a merchant with whom she had three children. The husband died in Galveston, Texas, in 1880; Hanna stayed for ten more years before she returned to Germany. She died in Würzburg in 1926.[24]

In 1878, when he was only fifteen years old, Seligmann's son Benzion (Zion) Lehmann emigrated to the United States as his uncles had done thirty years before. In 1882, he was followed by his brother Adolph, also fifteen years of age.[25] Benzion and Adolph decided to leave Germany at a time of economic crisis. As a result of the Franco-Prussian War of 1870/71, the German Empire had been created. After a short surge, the German economy lapsed into a long-lasting depression. Again the number of emigrants exploded. Altogether one and a half million Germans left for oversees countries between 1871 and 1885, 95 percent for the United States.[26] Like his sister Hanna, Benzion went to Texas, where he lived for thirty years.[27] There may be a connection with the fact that Lehman, Abraham & Co of New Orleans owned two cotton mills and real estate in Texas.[28] Benzion died in Würzburg in 1911 and was buried in the Jewish cemetery of Heidingsfeld. Adolph was living in Memphis, Tennessee, in 1892.[29] Nothing is known of his later life.

For many years, Mayer and Emanuel Lehman managed the affairs of Lehman Brothers alone. In the words of his son Herbert, Mayer was "very courageous in business," even "quite speculative." Emanuel was just the opposite, a very cautious man. The saying in the family was: "Mayer made the money, and Emanuel conserved the money." Despite these obvious differences of personality, they were extremely close in affection. Until the early nineties, they never had separate accounts in the office. It was always a joint fund on which either brother could draw when money was needed, and there was no accounting. According to his son, Mayer never took an important step in business without consulting with his wife, Babette, who had a keen and practical mind. Actually, Herbert remembered his mother as "definitely the head of the family": "She was as near the general impression of a matriarch as anybody I've ever known," he remarked.[30]

Emanuel Lehman (Herbert H. Lehman Suite and Papers, Columbia University, New York)

In 1870, Mayer Lehman, together with 131 other cotton merchants, organized the New York Cotton Exchange. He was on the first board of governors and head of its first finance committee.[31] In 1880, Meyer H. Lehman, their deceased brother Henry's eldest son, became a junior partner in Lehman Brothers. Sigmund M. Lehman, firstborn son of Mayer, was made a partner in 1882; his brothers Arthur and Herbert followed in 1901 and 1908, respectively. Philip, the only child of Emanuel to enter the business, became a partner in 1885.[32]

Mayer Lehman died at the age of sixty-seven on June 21, 1897, at his home after an operation performed for gangrene. Three days later, funeral services were held at Temple Emanu-El by Rabbi Gustav Gottheil. Upon learning of Mayer's death, the New York Cotton Exchange held a special meeting on June 23. During the funeral, the Exchange was closed for one hour, a mark of respect unique in the history of the institution up to that time.[33]

In Mayer's honor, Louis R. Ehrich wrote a poem that deserves to be quoted:

"A noble, manly, wide-beloved man!
He was not born unto a home of wealth,
Nor was he blest with opportunity
To train his mind by much of what the schools
Could teach. He came from sturdy, simple folk,
Who gave as heritage sound health, sound brain
And all the virtue of an honest name.
At time of life when other youths still lean
Upon their father's arm, or pleasure's voice
Pursue, he came across the mighty deep
To win his fortune in a country strange.
Two elder brothers bade him welcome here.
The one, alas! soon closed his eyes in sleep
That never ends. The other brother walked
With him in tread and step so evenly
That half a century passed before their march
Was broken and disturbed by cruel death.
He spurned all arts of trickery and deceit.
His word was seal enough. He did not build
His fortune on the ruin of other men.
With prudent care and self-denying life
He slowly added to his well-earned wealth.
Nor did his wealth beget false pride or stir
The promptings of a vain conceit. He was
Unto the very last a man of rare
And simplest modesty...[34]

When Mayer's son Herbert joined Lehman Brothers in 1908, control of the firm was in the hands of the second generation. Emanuel, who retired soon after Mayer's death, died in 1907 at the age of eighty. At that time, all partners were still members of the family. Under Herbert, Philip, Arthur, and Meyer H. Lehman, the business altered its character. During the first decades, Lehman Brothers was mainly occupied with trading in basic commodities like sugar, grain, cotton, petroleum, and coffee. Gradually the firm undertook large ventures in financing, both on its own account and for a growing clientele. Stock and bond transactions increased; in

1887, the firm acquired a seat on the New York Stock Exchange. Apart from representing the State of Alabama in the North, selling Alabama state bonds, Lehman Brothers helped finance the development of the South (railroads, textile mills, iron companies). Among the earliest of their ventures was the Tallassee Falls Manufacturing Company, a cotton mill near Montgomery, incorporated in 1878 with Mayer and Emanuel as directors.[35] At about the same time, the firm bought an interest in a similar Louisiana factory, the Lane Cotton Mills. In and about New York, they helped organize large banks and trust companies and took part in the formation of gas, ferry, and traction companies.[36]

Later, Lehman Brothers took a leading role in financing and advising the largest companies in the distributive industry of the United States. In 1906, together with another bank, they sold the public a considerable amount of stock in Sears, Roebuck. In 1912, they underwrote security issues for the F. W. Woolworth Company.[37] The firm had a close connection with the development of the department store in the United States. In 1950, Lehman Brothers declared: "Of today's twenty largest retailing enterprises, Lehman Brothers has been or is presently regarded as investment broker of more than half."[38] To name but two, the House of Lehman acted as financial advisors for R. H. Macy & Co. and Gimbel Brothers.[39]

The firm also financed one chain of department stores in Germany. Lehman Brothers at one time had about $100,000 in Reich money deposited in a German bank. After the inflation of 1922/23, only a tiny sum was left. The German bank stopped sending statements to New York and, when asked why, answered: "The stamp that we must put on a letter to you costs more than the whole account is now worth."[40]

During the twenties, the management of Lehman Brothers changed fundamentally. For the first time since its foundation, partners from outside the family were admitted. The leaders of the firm after Philip's retirement were Arthur Lehman and Philip's son, Robert.[41]

[1] Ashkenazi, *Business*, p. 28.

[2] Eric Foner, *Reconstruction. America's Unfinished Revolution, 1863-1877*, New York, 1989, p. 124.

[3] Elliott Ashkenazi, "Jewish Commercial Interests Between North and South: The Case of the Lehmans and the Seligmans," in *American Jewish Archives*, vol. XLIII, No. 1, Spring/Summer 1991, pp. 33-35; *Centennial*, pp. 19-20.

[4] Two years later, Emanuel Lehman visited Europe again. On July 2, 1869, he reached Baltimore on the steamer *Berlin*, whose port of embarkation had been Bremen; National Archives Microfilm Publications, Microcopy No. 255, *Passenger Lists of Vessels Arriving in Baltimore 1820-1891*, Roll 17.

[5] This was to remain the firm's office for nearly a decade, until it moved to larger quarters at 40 Exchange Place in 1876; *Centennial*, pp. 14-15.

[6] Herbert H. Lehman, *Reminiscences*, p. 5.

[7] Ferdinand Goldsmith had investments in the Indian Hill factory and the Lane Cotton Mills in New Orleans, both controlled by the Lehmans; Nevins, p. 12; Ashkenazi, *Business*, pp. 128-131.

8 The Stern family lives in Liverpool to this day. The family firm, Stern Bros., continues in the cotton business and recently has made a joint venture with one of the great cotton firms of America in Montgomery, Weil Bros. David Stern, a great-grandson of Abraham Stern, has recently retired as chairman of the Liverpool Cotton Exchange. Several years ago, he served for a year as honorary sheriff of Cheshire County, England. John L. Loeb, Jr. (letter to the author, September 27, 1995).

9 Ashkenazi, *Business*, pp. 129-132; Ashkenazi, *Commercial Interests*, p. 35; Herbert H. Lehman, *Reminiscences*, pp. 6-7; Newgass family tree. Maurice Stern and his family and descendants became prominent citizens of New Orleans. Almost 125 years later, Maurice Stern's grandson, Edgar Stern, and his great-grandson, Lessing Stern, became major shareholders of Deer Valley, one of the great ski resorts in Utah. Deer Valley is a major tenant of the United Park City Mines Company, which is controlled today by John L. Loeb and John L. Loeb, Jr. Through his mother, John L. Loeb, Jr., is a great-grandson of Babette Newgass. John L. Loeb, Jr. (letter to the author, September 27, 1995).

10 Newgass family tree; Birmingham, p. 70. A family legend has often been repeated in the Lehman family, namely, that Babette's and Esther's marriages to Mayer Lehman and Isaiah Hellman were arranged by their families in Germany. Babette was originally to marry Mr. Hellman, and Esther was to marry Mayer Lehman. But Esther got a sty in her eye and, as Mayer Lehman's marriage had been arranged before Mr. Hellman's, Babette was sent in her place. A hundred years later, Isaiah Hellman's great-grandson, Warren Hellman, became a partner of Lehman Brothers in New York. He now heads his own investment banking firm in San Francisco by the name of Hellman and Friedman. John L. Loeb, Jr. (letter to the author, September 27, 1995).

11 Therese, born in 1843, married Bernhard Steinheimer of Lohr. In 1889, the couple moved to Würzburg; in 1902, they were living in Bamberg. Their son Benno (born in Lohr in 1869) emigrated to England where he called himself Benno Stoneham. Bernhard's and Therese's daughter Lina (born in 1872) married a man named William Silberman. Newgass family tree; Strätz, *Biographisches Handbuch*, II. Teilband, p. 589. For Babette's other sisters, Helena (Hannchen) and Klara, see below.

12 B. Guiness Orchard, *Liverpool's Legion of Honour*, Liverpool, 1893, p. 601.

13 Ashkenazi, *Commercial Interests*, p. 35.

14 Joseph Rosenheim died in 1888; his eldest son, twenty-one-year-old Felix, became the working head of L. Rosenheim & Sons, cotton and commission merchants. In 1893, the firm had clients or representatives in nearly every European country; *Liverpool's Legion of Honour*, pp. 601-602. Benjamin Newgass, owner of B. Newgass & Co, went to London; his last entry in the Liverpool Street Directory appeared in 1885. Information provided by the Liverpool Record Office (letter to the author, January 23, 1995).

15 Birmingham, p. 289; Morgenthau, p. 38; Nevins, pp. 22-24; Rosenheim and Lehman family tree.

16 Herbert H. Lehman, *Reminiscences*, p. 5.

17 Clara married a man named Richard Limburg with whom she had three children. Arthur became a partner in Lehman Brothers in 1901. He was a longtime president of the New York Federation of Jewish Philanthropies and a member of the board of trustees of the New School for Social Research and of the Museum of the City of New York. Arthur married Adele Lewisohn, whose father Adolph had been born in Hamburg and who had emigrated to the USA in 1867. Adolph Lewisohn made a fortune in the mining business and devoted much of his wealth to cultural and philanthropic causes. Lewisohn was from an extremely old Danish/German Jewish family. His great-great-grandfather was Nachman Joachim Levy of Rendsburg, then part of Denmark. Direct descendants of Nachman Joachim Levy include the Hambro family of Denmark, Norway, and England. Arthur Lehman's daughter Frances became a prominent civic leader in New York and, for more than a decade, was the commissioner of the City of New York to the United Nations; she married John L. Loeb, head of the investment banking house Loeb, Rhoades. Her sister Helen married Benjamin Buttenwieser, a partner in the banking firm Kuhn, Loeb. From 1949 to 1951, Benjamin served as deputy high commissioner for Germany under High Commissioner John McCloy. Helen was a distinguished attorney and the first woman chairman of the Legal Aid Society. Genealogical Record of the Mayer Lehman Family, 1778-1961, compiled by

Edith and Herbert Lehman; Bo Bramsen, Kathleen Wain, *The Hambros: 1779-1979*, London, 1979; Lehman Family Reunion Press Release; Nevins, p. 398; Birmingham, p. 377; John L. Loeb, Jr. (letter to the author, September 27, 1995).

[18] John L. Loeb, Jr. (letter to the author, March 7, 1995); I. S. Meyer, *Catalogue of the Jewish Art Objects in the Collection of Judge Irving Lehman*, 1932, No. 26.

[19] Herbert H. Lehman, *Reminiscences*, pp. 10, 19; Babette Lehman, letter to Herbert H. Lehman (March 26, 1898), made available by the Herbert H. Lehman Suite and Papers, Columbia University, New York.

[20] Many members of the second and third generations abandoned religious practices, and, for example, had Christmas trees instead of celebrating Hanukkah. Margaret Josten, granddaughter of Mayer and Babette Lehman, described one particular visit of her grandmother: "I can remember when we had our first Christmas tree. Grandma Lehman was coming to call on us, and we were all scared that she would be furious. Aunt Clara (Mayer and Babette's daughter Clara Limburg) had had one the year before. She always did things first. But no one had dared tell Grandma. When she came in, we all held our breath. At first she didn't say anything. Then she looked at the tree and turned to my mother and said: 'Isn't it lovely?' We were all terribly relieved." Morgenthau, p. xiv.

[21] Herbert H. Lehman, *Reminiscences*, pp. 20-21; *In Memoriam. Mayer Lehman*, New York 1897, p. 20; Birmingham, p. 131; Nevins, p. 25.

[22] Herbert H. Lehman, *Reminiscences*, pp. 19-20; *In Memoriam. Mayer Lehman*, pp. 11, 18, 21-27.

[23] Herbert H. Lehman, *Reminiscences*, pp. 536-537. For social discrimination in nineteenth century Würzburg cf. Flade, *Die Würzburger Juden*, and Gehring-Münzel, *Schutzjude*, passim.

[24] Würzburg City Archives, Einwohnermeldeamt, Meldebogen Hanna (Hannchen) Northmann. Two of Hanna's children died early: Arthur in 1893 at the age of seventeen, Lilly in 1903 at the age of twenty-five. The third child, daughter Addie, married a lawyer in Mainz.

[25] Würzburg State Archives, Regierung von Unterfranken 14066, 14071.

[26] Wust, Moos (eds.), p. 46.

[27] Legend on Benzion's headstone in Heidingsfeld's Jewish cemetery.

[28] *Centennial*, p. 7; Ashkenazi, *Business*, p. 129.

[29] Last will and testament of Zion M. Lehman, June 30, 1892; State of Alabama Department of Archives and History, Montgomery County Will Book 8.

[30] Herbert H. Lehman, *Reminiscences*, pp. 13, 17-18.

[31] Ashkenazi, *Commercial Interests*, p. 35.

[32] Meyer devoted himself entirely to cotton and coffee trading until his retirement in 1904. Philip's partnership continued until his death in 1947. Arthur played an important role in the firm until he died in 1936; *Centennial*, pp. 15-16.

[33] *In Memoriam. Mayer Lehman*, pp. 4, 8-9, 12-16, 20.

[34] *In Memoriam. Maier Lehman*, p. 3.

[35] In 1897, a new mill was erected. At that time, the board of directors of the Tallassee Falls Manufacturing Company included Emanuel and Mayer Lehman, John W. Durr, J. Spencer Turner, Maurice Stern, and Sigmund Roman, a son of the Lehmans' sister Nanne. Virginia Noble Golden, *A History of Tallassee for Tallasseeans*, 1949, p. 42.

[36] *Centennial*, pp. 18-24.

[37] Nevins, p. 49.

[38] *Centennial*, p. 46.

[39] Nevins, p. 62.

[40] Herbert H. Lehman, *Reminiscences*, pp. 200-201, 537; Nevins, p. 64.

[41] Nevins, pp. 64-65.

Chapter Ten

Herbert H. Lehman
and Franklin D. Roosevelt

Herbert Henry Lehman was born on March 28, 1878, in New York, the eighth and last child of Mayer and Babette Lehman. He was named in honor of Mayer's brother, Henry, who had died in 1855, and of his father's close friend, Hilary A. Herbert, an attorney in Montgomery who went to Washington as a member of the House of Representatives and became secretary of the navy under President Grover Cleveland in 1893.[1]

Before he was ten years old, Herbert had traveled to Europe twice with his parents. They visited his mother's sister, Betti, in Liverpool and her brother, Benjamin, in London. In 1886, Benjamin Newgass had left Liverpool; in true Lehman fashion, his cotton business stayed within the family. Abraham Stern, husband of his sister Betti, took over and B. Newgass & Co became A. Stern & Co in 1886.[2] Benjamin, according to his nephew, Herbert H. Lehman, was an extremely speculative man: "He made and lost several fortunes. Whenever he saw anything cheap, he could not resist it. A lace store in Venice, for example, might be for sale at a bargain. He took possession, though he had no idea what he could do with it."[3] When he died on September 8, 1921, Benjamin Newgass left a fortune of 228,000 pounds. In his will he requested his five children "to continue to interest themselves in the same Jewish and other charities for which I have worked, and to do so both with their time, and energy, and their means."[4]

Whenever he came to Europe, Herbert visited his grandmother, Friederike Neugaß, in Würzburg and spent many weeks with her. As a youth he spoke German well. Even as an old man he read it fluently and spoke enough German to make himself fairly well understood.[5] Until her death in 1908, at the age of ninety-two, Friederike lived in Würzburg in an apartment on Augustinerstraße. Together with her husband, Isaak, and her youngest child, Klara, she had moved from Rieneck to Würzburg in 1868, seven years after the *Matrikelparagraph*, the most hated part of the Jewish Edict, had been abolished and Bavarian Jews were at last allowed to settle where they wished. The family was not alone in coming to Würzburg; by 1880, 2,271 Jews were living in the city, compared to 496 three decades earlier.[6]

Klara Neugaß died in 1872, only twenty-one years old. Isaak Neugaß passed away three years later, at the age of seventy-three.[7] As Würzburg's Jewish cemetery was only opened in 1882,[8] both Klara and Isaak (and later Friederike) were buried in the Jewish cemetery of Heidingsfeld,[9] also the burial place of Abraham Lehmann. But while it is impossible to find Abraham's grave, the headstones on Friederike and Isaak Neugaß's graves are intact and easy to see.

79

Augustinerstraße in Würzburg around the turn of the century (Würzburg City Archives)

In his 1957 conversation with Wendell Link and Prof. Joseph Wall of the Oral History Research Office of Columbia University, Herbert Lehman mentioned one particular visit to Würzburg and his grandmother in 1884 that he never forgot: "When my parents used to go to Carlsbad - my father used to take the cure there - they'd always leave me with my grandmother and aunts. I remember it distinctly because I never got over the gratitude I felt to my one aunt. In those days, they treated little boys in many ways like little girls. I mean, the boys had curls and they wore skirts until they were six or seven years old, and I was always very much distressed about that, very much ashamed. I had curls. This aunt of mine, who was a very, very forceful woman with very definite views of her own, ... didn't approve at all of my having curls at the age of six. When my mother left me in her charge, she took me to the barber and had my curls cut off. It was one of the happiest experiences of my life. I remember when my mother came back, she cried, because her little baby boy - I was her baby boy at that time - ceased to have curls. When she died we found in her effects one of the locks of my hair wrapped up in tissue paper."[10]

The aunt mentioned here is Babette Newgass's sister, Helena (Hannchen). In 1860, she had married Sondel Stern, a cattle dealer of Heßdorf; the childless couple later moved to Würzburg, where Sondel died in 1912. In 1921, five years before her own death, Hannchen made an endowment under the name of *Mayer und Babette Lehmann-Wohltätigkeitsstiftung* ("Mayer and Babette Lehmann Charity Fund") to the city of Würzburg. The interests on the capital of 100,000 marks were to be spent on needy Würzburg Jews.[11] Maybe the money had come from America.

In 1884, Mayer's brother Seligmann, who lived in Heidingsfeld, was still alive, and the Lehmans from America most certainly paid him a visit, too. Seligmann died in 1890.[12]

In 1887, Mayer's family made another European trip. In London, they witnessed Queen Victoria's Golden Jubilee, and Herbert remembered the throngs that filled the streets and the parades. Herbert came to Europe again in 1897, 1902, and 1906. "We went over every three or four years," he said later.[13] The family visited Europe shortly after the Dreyfus trial. In 1894, Captain Alfred Dreyfus, an Alsatian Jewish officer on the French General Staff, had been courtmartialed for treason, degraded, and sentenced to imprisonment on Devil's Island. Dreyfus was pardoned in 1899, acquitted in 1906, and readmitted to the army. This case of obvious anti-Jewish bias drove Theodor Herzl to publish his Zionist platform *Der Judenstaat* in 1896. Herbert Lehman, however, never became a Zionist, although he could sympathize with the emotion behind Zionist aspirations.

When his father died in 1897, Herbert was a student at Williams College in Massachusetts. During his school vacations, he lived with his mother in the family house on Sixty-Second Street. By 1902, all his brothers and sisters had married; Babette sold the house and moved to an apartment house at 175 West 58th Street. Herbert stayed with her until he also married in 1910.[14]

Even as a youth, growing up in the affluent, closely-knit society of successful German-Jewish families, Herbert developed an interest in social reform. As a student of Dr. Julius Sachs's Collegiate Institute for Boys, he visited the so-called great ghetto of the Lower East Side, where impoverished Jewish immigrants from Eastern Europe lived in great squalor. "The poverty and the filth and the bleakness"[15] impressed him deeply. Later, he was attracted to Lillian Wald, a nurse who taught the immigrant families diet and sanitation and cared for the ill. She became his lifelong friend and influenced his thinking on social matters. In 1895, Lillian Wald moved to 265 Henry Street and, together with other nurses, made the "Henry Street Settlement" a center of self-help for immigrant families with courses in home nursing, cooking, and sewing, with boys' and girls' clubs organizing recreational activities and presenting programs in music, dramatics, and arts.[16]

When he was a student at Williams, Herbert came to know Lillian Wald better, and shortly after his graduation in 1899 he became responsible for a group of boys aged twelve to fourteen. He kept up his work in the Henry Street Settlement for about four years, gaining a deep insight into slum problems. Actually, as Henry Morgenthau III has observed, Henry Street, operated mainly by sons and daughters of established Jewish families, was a kind of social service finishing school for

The Herbert Lehman Family

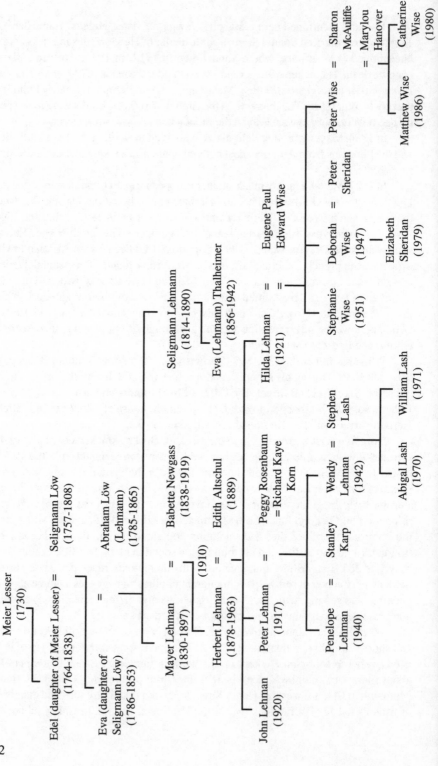

Herbert H. Lehman (left) and his brother Irving in 1884, when the former was six and the latter was eight years old (Herbert H. Lehman Suite and Papers, Columbia University, New York)

those who aspired to careers in public life. At the turn of the century, 90,000 Jews were arriving in the city every year, most of them from Russia and Poland. Almost a million Jews lived in New York by then, about a quarter of the total population.[17]

Herbert Lehman kept some of the letters his parents wrote to him during his Williams years. Surprisingly, they are all in German, which gives us a clue about the language spoken in the Lehman home when the family members were among themselves. Babette and Mayer, four decades after their emigration, probably used their native tongue in conversation with their sons and daughters. The children may have spoken English among themselves - Irving's messages to Herbert on his parents' letters are always in English - and they may not have been too happy with their parents' clinging to German. In one of his letters, Mayer apologizes for not writing earlier, citing Herbert's dislike "of my German" as a reason.[18]

One of Mayer's letters, written on September 27, 1895, when Herbert had just entered Williams, contains the father's request to consider him his "best, most intimate friend" in case Herbert ever got himself into trouble, signed "your devoted father Mayer." Babette wrote more often, keeping her son informed about family matters, entreating him time and again to dress warmly to avoid a cold and to smoke only moderately or not at all. After Mayer's death, Babette expressed her desire "that through you, my dear children, the name of Mayer Lehman may be and remain in honor" (*daß durch Euch liebe Kinder der Name von Mayer Lehman stets ein geachteter sein und bleiben wird*). On the occasion of his twenty-first birthday, she asked of her youngest son to consider in all his actions what his father would have advised him to do.

Upon graduation, Herbert entered the cotton goods business as a salesman with the J. Spencer Turner Company in New York. He was so successful that by 1906, at the age of twenty-eight, he had become vice president and treasurer of the company. Two years later, he joined Lehman Brothers as a partner. On April 28, 1910, he married Edith Altschul, the twenty-year-old daughter of a banker.[19] Having no sons and daughters of their own, Herbert and Edith adopted three children: Peter (born in 1917), John (1920), and Hilda (1921).[20]

In 1914, the First World War broke out; Herbert Lehman advocated American entry long before the government did. When the United States finally declared war on Germany in 1917, he desperately wanted to take part in the fighting, but, despite his efforts, was not called. He went to Washington instead and worked for the Navy Bureau of Supplies and Accounts. It was there that he met and made a friend of Franklin D. Roosevelt, then assistant secretary of the navy. Later, Herbert played a leading role in supervising the supplies for the whole army. For his outstanding work, he was awarded the Distinguished Service Medal. In mid-1919, Herbert Lehman retired from active service as a colonel on the General Staff and rejoined Lehman Brothers.[21]

At the very beginning of the First World War, Herbert, together with his brother Arthur and a group of distinguished American Jews, founded the Jewish Joint Distribution Committee (JDC), a relief organization for the Jewish population of war-torn Europe. $16,500,000 was raised; food, clothing, medicines, and funds were distributed, mostly in the countries of Eastern Europe. After the armistice, turmoil and civic conflict enveloped Eastern Europe. In Poland and the Ukraine, anti-Jewish riots surfaced. During pogroms, several hundred thousands of Jews lost their lives.

The "Joint," as it became known, together with other relief organizations, fed countless starving European Jews. In the years 1919 and 1920, the JDC raised another $27,000,000, a work in which Herbert Lehman was prominent. During the twenties, the Joint concentrated on rebuilding Jewish communities in Europe and training people in self-help. Schools and other cultural centers were reorganized; a war against disease was conducted. Herbert, who himself gave substantial sums, was chairman of a JDC subcommittee responsible for the economic rehabilitation of Jewish communities from the Baltic to the Black Sea. By 1924, he had also become vice chairman of the JDC itself.[22]

Among the 1,800 educational institutions in Europe that the "Joint" helped maintain was the Jewish Teachers Seminary (*Israelitische Lehrerbildungsanstalt*) in Würzburg. When, due to the inflation in Germany, contributions to the seminary dropped drastically in 1924, the "Joint" helped out. Three years earlier, the JDC had provided poor Würzburg Jews with passover matzoh.[23]

Herbert Lehman's social activities were widespread. He was a director of the Welfare Council of New York City, of the Child Welfare Committee of America, and the National Association for the Advancement of Colored People. He also acted as vice chairman of the Palestine Economic Corporation, and as trustee of the Hebrew Sheltering Guardian Society and the Bureau of Jewish Social Research.[24]

Franklin D. Roosevelt is sworn in as governor of the State of New York on December 31, 1928. From left: Edith Lehman, Lieutenant Governor Herbert H. Lehman, Judge Irving Lehman, Franklin D. Roosevelt, and Eleanor Roosevelt. (Herbert H. Lehman Suite and Papers, Columbia University, New York)

From the time he left Williams College, Herbert Lehman became well known in Democratic party circles. As early as 1920, he was one of the staunch supporters of New York Governor Al Smith. In 1924, Smith appointed him to mediate industrial disputes in the garment trades. In 1926, New York Mayor James J. Walker commissioned Lehman to study the city's finances. During Al Smith's campaign for the presidency in 1928, he acted as National Democratic Committee finance chairman. Herbert Lehman ran for lieutenant governor of the State of New York in that year with Franklin D. Roosevelt as the candidate for governor. Both were elected by a small margin, while Smith was crushingly defeated by Herbert C. Hoover in the presidential race.[25]

Heidingsfeld's synagogue after the restoration of 1929. Notice the shrine in which the torah scrolls were kept (left), the raised platform in the center (bimah) with a desk for the reading of the torah scroll, and the women's gallery. The brass chandeliers are from the 16th and 17th centuries. (Walter Obst, Würzburg)

As soon as he was elected, Herbert Lehman resigned from Lehman Brothers and severed all active business association. During his first year in office, Roosevelt was often away in Warm Springs, Georgia, pursuing recovery from polio, an illness he had first contracted in 1921. Whenever his friend left New York, Herbert became acting governor, with full power to meet any emergency. Even when he was in the state, Roosevelt delegated many tasks to "the other governor," as he called him. In particular, Herbert Lehman took over from Roosevelt physically taxing duties of travel and inspection.

From the very beginning, prison reform was high on the governor's and his deputy's list of priorities. After a riot had broken out in the state prison of Auburn, Lehman initiated far-reaching reforms. Semisecure penitentiaries were put in operation for prisoners who were not actually dangerous, and a new boys' reformatory was built, offering better vocational training. In addition, the parole system was changed. When Lieutenant Governor Lehman made a personal investigation of the state hospitals for mental patients, he was shocked by their deplorable state. Within a relatively short time, overcrowding was reduced by building additions to existing facilities.[26]

After the stock market crash in the fall of 1929 and the onset of the Great Depression, emergency relief for the growing number of jobless gained first priority on Roosevelt's and Lehman's agenda. Large programs for public work were instituted. In the following year, the governor and his deputy scored a landslide victory in the gubernatorial election.[27] Also in 1929, the synagogue of Heidingsfeld, home of Herbert Lehman's great-great-grandfather Meier Lesser, was restored to its original splendor. At the opening ceremony of the redecorated building, Heidingsfeld's mayor praised the devotion of Bavaria's Jews who had raised the necessary sum in a community effort.[28]

When Roosevelt became the Democratic candidate for the presidency in 1932, it was logical that Herbert Lehman would succeed him as governor. Lehman astonished even his most enthusiastic supporters by reaching the unheard of plurality of 849,000 votes. On the same day, Franklin Roosevelt defeated incumbent president Herbert Hoover.[29] Rimpar and Heidingsfeld and the whole governmental district of Lower Franconia took notice of Lehman's triumph. The *Würzburger General-Anzeiger*, Lower Franconia's leading daily newspaper, published an article exhibiting pride in the fact that Lehman's father had emigrated from the Würzburg region. "The new governor of New York and his Würzburg connection," the headline read on November 11, 1932, less than three months before Adolf Hitler's rise to power. The article mentioned several visits Herbert had paid to Würzburg and stressed the fact that each time he had stayed for weeks.[30]

On January 2, 1933, the inauguration of the new governor took place in the assembly chamber in Albany. In his inaugural address, Herbert Lehman promised to care for the unemployed, needy, and helpless and to broaden the sphere of government for social ends. Indeed, drastic steps had to be taken: in the State of New York, 1,750,000 people were out of work. As governor, Herbert Lehman, against heavy opposition, put into effect a welfare system and a program for unemployment insurance that became models for the national and other state governments. In 1935, the legislature passed the first bill for a state unemployment insurance. It only protected unemployed wage earners for thirteen weeks, but marked an important beginning. The *New York Herald Tribune* commented on the 1935 legislatory process with these words: "Not in years has so much legislation backed by the American Federation of Labor gone through Albany." George Meany of the AFL described the legislation as the most enlightened, humane, and progressive ever enacted in any state.[31] In 1934, Herbert Lehman was reelected by an overwhelming majority. In the fall elections of 1936, he and Roosevelt again scored sweeping victories. In 1938, Lehman, after a change in the state constitution, was reelected for a four-year term.[32]

One year later, Herbert's brother Irving was to become chief justice of the New York State Court of Appeals. Irving had studied at Columbia University. In 1898, he was admitted to the bar; he practised his profession until 1908, when he was elected for a fourteen-year term as a justice of the New York Supreme Court. In

1922, he was renominated for a second judicial term of office. After another year, he was elected as associate judge of the New York State Court of Appeals, the highest court in the state; in 1939, he became chief justice. For the first time in the history of any state of the United States, two brothers headed two coordinate branches of the government, the executive and the judicial.

Irving Lehman's administration of justice followed modern progressive judicial thought. Thus he prepared a strong dissenting opinion in a case wherein the majority of the New York Court of Appeals held that legislation establishing minimum wage standards was unconstitutional. To his (and his brother's) satisfaction, Irving saw the court eventually overrule its decision.[33] Judge Lehman was an active member of the Jewish Welfare Board, president of Temple Emanu-El from 1929 to 1938, and served on the executive committee of the Union of American Hebrew Congregations. A scholar in Hebraic culture, he was active in the promotion of Jewish religious education and cultural interests. To Irving Lehman, the basic concept of religious freedom appealed as the very foundation of individual liberties: "True freedom (he wrote) was not achieved so long as thought and conscience might be fettered. ... As the very foundation of our government, the organic law decrees freedom of thought and conscience, yet from time to time men try to destroy or abridge the freedom which the law decrees. It has been said that no man is worthy of freedom who cannot defend it. ... We rejoice and are proud because we are citizens of the country which has recognized that right (religious freedom) and guaranteed it in its constitution. We prove ourselves worthy of it when we are ready to defend it from direct or indirect attack, when we fight all forms of prejudice, whether directed against us or others, which threaten it."[34]

[1] Herbert H. Lehman, *Reminiscences*, p. 1; Nevins, pp. 13, 20.

[2] David Stern, Liverpool (letter to John L. Loeb, Jr., April 4, 1995).

[3] Nevins, p. 9. In London, Benjamin was president of the Atlantic and Danville Railway Company and a director of the Cardinal Investment Trust, Columbia Railways and Navigation Company, San Luis (Mexico); *Post and Mercury*, Liverpool, July 5, 1922.

[4] *Post and Mercury*, Liverpool, July 5, 1922. According to the newspaper, Benjamin Newgass had been a member of the Anglo-Jewish Association for many years. Benjamin married twice. With his first wife, Sarah Beer, he had two daughters (Bettie and Cecily); with his second wife Maria he had three sons (Edgar, Gerald, and Harold). Maria died in 1942; Newgass family tree.

[5] Herbert H. Lehman, *Reminiscences*, pp. 21-23.

[6] Flade, *Juden in Würzburg*, p. 21.

[7] Würzburg City Archives, Einwohnermeldeamt, Meldebogen Isaak Neugaß.

[8] Flade, *Würzburger Juden*, p. 154.

[9] Würzburg State Archives, Jüdische Standesregister 41, 42.

[10] Herbert H. Lehman, *Reminiscences*, pp. 22-23.

[11] Würzburg City Archives, Einwohnermeldeamt, Meldebögen Sondel Stern, Hannchen Stern; *Würzburger General-Anzeiger*, October 5, 1921, p. 2. The whole sum was lost during the inflation of 1923.

[12] Würzburg State Archives, Jüdische Standesregister 42.

[13] Herbert H. Lehman, *Reminiscences*, p. 23; Nevins, pp. 28-29.

[14] Herbert H. Lehman, *Reminiscences*, p. 19. Babette Lehman died on August 25, 1919.

[15] Herbert H. Lehman, *Reminiscences*, p. 30.

[16] Herbert H. Lehman, *Reminiscences*, p. 31; Nevins, pp. 30-31.

[17] Morgenthau, pp. 216-217; Birmingham, p. 289; Nevins, pp. 77-78.

[18] All letters were kindly provided by the Herbert H. Lehman Suite and Papers, Columbia University, New York.

[19] Nevins, pp. 41-42, 51.

[20] Genealogical Record of the Mayer Lehman Family.

[21] Herbert H. Lehman, *Reminiscences*, p. 8; Nevins, pp. 55-62.

[22] Nevins, pp. 68-73.

[23] Flade, *Juden in Würzburg*, pp. 173, 200; Walter H. Kaufman, "A History of the Jewish Teachers Seminary in Würzburg (ILBA)," in Max Ottensoser, Alex Roberg (eds.), *ILBA. Israelitische Lehrerbildungsanstalt Würzburg, 1864-1938, by the Alumni of 1930-1938*, Huntington Woods, Michigan, 1982, p. 46.

[24] *Universal Jewish Encyclopedia*, vol. 6, p. 594.

[25] Nevins, pp. 85-106.

[26] Nevins, pp. 108-109, 115-117.

[27] Nevins, pp. 116, 122-127.

[28] "Einweihung der wiederhergestellten Synagoge in Heidingsfeld", in *Bayerische Israelitische Gemeindezeitung*, October 15, 1929, pp. 331-332. Cf. Central Archives for the History of the Jewish People, Jerusalem, WR 449a.

[29] Nevins, pp. 127, 131; *Universal Jewish Encyclopedia*, vol. 6, p. 594.

[30] "Der neue Gouverneur von New York und seine Beziehungen zu Würzburg," in *Würzburger General-Anzeiger*, November 11, 1932, p. 3.

[31] Nevins, pp. 132-134, 167.

[32] Nevins, pp. 172, 177, 196.

[33] *Universal Jewish Encyclopedia*, vol. 6, pp. 595-596; Nevins, p. 205.

[34] Irving Lehman was also a member of the board of governors of the American Friends of the Hebrew University in Jerusalem and a member of the board of directors of the Jewish Theological Seminary of America. *Universal Jewish Encyclopedia*, vol. 6, p. 596.

Chapter Eleven

The Lehmans
and the Tragedy of German Jewry

Among American leaders, Herbert Lehman certainly was one of the best-informed about European matters. Still, like most others in Germany and abroad, he was unable to foresee the atrocities committed during the "Third Reich." Herbert had visited Germany at the time of Foreign Secretary Walther Rathenau's murder and had witnessed severe right-wing disturbances.[1] One year later, in 1923, Adolf Hitler attempted to overthrow the Bavarian government in Munich. "Almost immediately after Hitler started his rise, I became very, very fearful," Lehman said later.[2] During his years as governor, he continued to keep a close look at Germany and the fate of German Jews.

It should be noted that Lower Franconia with its predominantly Catholic population had given the *Nationalsozialistische Deutsche Arbeiterpartei* (NSDAP) the smallest percentage of support in all of Bavaria before Hitler came to power. As of January 1, 1933, the district had the lowest proportion of its population enlisted as Nazi party members, not only in Bavaria, but out of all thirty-two districts across Germany.[3] This, of course, did not prevent Lower Franconia's NSDAP under its leader *(Gauleiter)*, Otto Hellmuth, a dentist, from fullheartedly joining in the nationwide campaign of harassment, started after the National Socialists seized power on January 30, 1933. The first period of Nazi terror was characterized by a highly charged atmosphere of street demonstrations, marches, and the takeover of local and state governments, accompanied by acts of violence perpetrated by the *Sturm-Abteilungen* (SA), which had been drafted as auxiliary police. This phase brought legislative exclusion of German Jews primarily from public life, including the removal of certain categories of civil servants.[4] The campaign's long-term aim was to alienate Jews from their neighbors, to push them out of villages and towns, and ultimately to push them out of Germany.[5]

Right from the start of the "Third Reich," the world's media concentrated on the brutal treatment German Jews were receiving. These well-founded reports infuriated the National Socialist government in Berlin, which tried to silence critical voices by calling a one-day boycott of Jewish shops, doctors, and lawyers on April 1, 1933. German Jews were only suffering from bad news abroad, the propaganda went, not from Nazi treatment itself. On March 29, 1933, the leaders of Würzburg's Jewish community congregated in the building next to the synagogue. In neighboring communities, Jews had indeed been mistreated, they knew. But, so far, this had not happened in Würzburg itself. There was no reason to lose hope, Gerson Haas, president of the congregation, remarked. After a prolonged discussion, the assembled men decided to send a telegram to Governor Lehman. The representatives of Würzburg's Jews asked Lehman to spread the news that members of their community were not being subjected to mistreatment.[6]

A Jewish man accused of having a sexual relationship with a non-Jewish woman is led through Würzburg's Kürschnerhof *(ca 1935) (Roland Flade Collection)*

When the governor planned to appear at a mass meeting at Madison Square Garden to protest anti-Jewish acts in Germany, he received a substantial number of telegrams from leading Jews in Germany urging him not to attend. The whole meeting should be given up, Lehman read in the cables, else it would further inflame Hitler. "It's perfectly evident that they were dispatched under (a) great sense of fear what would happen, and a great desire not to do anything that would possibly rock the boat," Lehman said later. "I know the great majority of the men who sent me these cables did not survive the war."[7]

Shortly after he got the telegram from Würzburg, the first Jews of that city were taken to concentration camps and killed.[8] By late 1933, in several villages across Lower Franconia, Jews were not permitted to live or work, or even to travel through on their way to another place.[9] The Nuremberg Laws of 1935 and subsequent *Verordnungen* led to the exclusion of all remaining Jewish civil servants and declared illegal all further marriages and sexual relations outside marriage between Jews and citizens of "German or kindred blood." Jews were deprived of German citizenship

91

rights. In 1936, the provincial president of Lower Franconia reported that, since the decreeing of the Nuremberg Laws, the Jews "are selling off their businesses and preparing themselves for emigration."[10]

Anti-Jewish activities culminated during the massive pogroms of *Kristallnacht* (November 9/10th, 1938) that followed the shooting of a German embassy official in Paris by a desperate seventeen-year-old Jewish boy. Houses and apartments of Jewish citizens were ransacked, stores looted, and synagogues desecrated and burnt down. Tens of thousands of Jewish men were taken prisoner and transported to the concentration camps of Dachau and Buchenwald; many were beaten to death. A number of German Jews committed suicide. At least three of these suicides happened in Würzburg.[11]

In Rimpar, home of Herbert Lehman's father and uncles, the interior of the synagogue was destroyed. The same happened in Rieneck, the village in which his mother had been born 101 years earlier.[12] The Heidingsfeld synagogue was higher than all surrounding buildings. In the words of an eyewitness it "looked like a huge torch in the hands of a giant when it was put to fire at 2:30 A.M. on November 10th."[13] "The recent atrocities surpass anything known in modern history," Herbert Lehman wrote to a friend shortly after the pogroms.[14]

In Rieneck, *Kristallnacht* started on November 10 in bright daylight. In the afternoon, SA men from Rieneck and neighboring villages forced their way into the house of forty-five-year-old Berthold Neugaß and his wife, Elsa. Until recently, Berthold had been a cattle dealer like his father Mendel before him. His brother had died as a German soldier during the First World War. Berthold's grandfather had been a brother of Isaak Neugaß.[15] Shortly after they entered the house, SA men were seen to throw household effects out of the windows. These were then burnt in the yard until this proved too dangerous for surrounding buildings. Around 4:30 P.M., when it started to get dark, most of what was still left was put onto a wagon and burnt outside Rieneck. The *Sturm-Abteilungen* confiscated 140 marks in cash and a radio. Some of the linen thrown out of a small window on the first floor fell into the garden; a few pieces got stuck in a tree. The members of Rieneck's three remaining Jewish families had to spend the night of November 10/11 in the house of one of these families near city hall. The other two houses were guarded by SA men. Now that the furniture and so much else had been destroyed, looting was to be prevented, a telling example of the perverted sense of justice that reigned during the "Third Reich." On the morning of November 11, Berthold Neugaß and his wife were allowed to return to their house. The first thing Berthold did was to remove the laundry that was still hanging in the tree. Later, the radio and the confiscated money were returned.[16]

Berthold and Elsa were left alone in their ransacked house for no more than three days. On November 15, Berthold was arrested again and taken to the public health officer in nearby Gemünden. Shivering, he stood in front of this man whose task it was to determine whether Neugaß was well enough to be sent to a concentration camp. From Gemünden, Berthold Neugaß was transported to Würzburg's prison, interrogated, and photographed. Afterward, he became one of the tens of thousands of inmates of the notorious Dachau concentration camp.

Berthold Neugaß of Rieneck is photographed in Würzburg prison on November 15, 1938 (Würzburg State Archives)

David Schuster, a young man from the Lower Franconian town of Bad Brückenau, has vividly described the beginning of his "protective custody" *(Schutzhaft)* in Dachau: "It was called baptism of fire *(Feuertaufe)*. The new arrivals were raked over the coals. After prison clothes had been distributed and everybody was registered, we were received by the *Oberführer*. 'Your custody is not a matter of days and months, but of years,' he said. He warned against attempts to escape. 'Who trespasses the line in front of the ditch and the barbed wire will be shot without warning,' he added. When he was ready, he said: *'Herr Wachtmeister,* practise some sport with these men!' It went like this: 'Double time, march! Lie down, stand up, face about! Double time, march! Lie down, stand up!' It was a terrible torture, through dirt and mud. When the *Wachtmeister* had had enough, we were led to rails: 'Pick up!' At first there were so many prisoners that, among constant kicking and yelling, we were able to lift the rails. Then one prisoner after another was called away until so few were left that they just had to give up. After that the SS men decided whom they were going to finish, maybe somebody with glasses or a man who looked like an intellectual, maybe a delicate man or a clumsy man. Some had to bite the dust on that very first day. Shortly after my arrival, a prisoner was slain in front of our eyes. A man who had spent some time in the camp said to me: 'If you get agitated over that, you will be their next victim. You have to think: better him than me. Otherwise you will not get over it.'"[17]

While Berthold Neugaß was a prisoner in Dachau, his house and real estate were sold to the town of Rieneck. As most of the documents necessary for his emigration to the United States were ready, he was released from Dachau on December 13. Upon his return to Rieneck, Berthold had to report to the local police station each Monday and Friday at 5 P.M.[18] In March 1939, all remaining thirteen Rieneck Jews moved to Frankfurt am Main.[19] It took another year, however, until Berthold and Elsa were able to leave Germany for America. In 1941, they were living in Newark, New Jersey.[20]

In stark contrast to the nineteenth century, America no longer welcomed all immigrants. Congress had passed restrictive immigration laws between 1917 and 1924 and amended them in 1929, introducing a system of "quotas" based on national origin. Before a quota immigrant was admitted, he had to prove that he was not "likely to become a public charge." Immigrants without adequate means to guarantee economic self-sufficiency were required to provide "affidavits of support" from relatives or close friends in the United States. These affidavits had to be accompanied by detailed proof of financial solvency. The immigration quota for German and Austrian nationals (including Jews) was fixed at 27,370 per year, comparable to the quota for the United Kingdom. Only about 6,000 persons were to be admitted each year from Italy or Poland, countries with large Catholic and Jewish populations whose immigration was judged undesirable by a majority of Congress.[21]

For several years, German immigration numbers stayed well below the quota, fluctuating between 1,450 in 1933 and 11,520 in 1937. There were a number of reasons for this: the hope of many Germans that the "Third Reich" would be short-lived; the severe economic conditions in the United States, which were not unknown to people wishing to emigrate; the widespread ignorance of the English language among Germans; and the time-consuming process of gathering the extensive proofs demanded by American immigration officials. During the 1930s, in a period of economic distress, efforts of Jewish and non-Jewish groups in the United States to persuade President Roosevelt and the Congress to liberalize immigration laws or admission procedures proved fruitless.[22] In 1935, Governor Lehman wrote to the president expressing his wish that American consular representatives in Germany show sympathetic interest in permitting immigration of German Jews into the United States. On November 13, 1935, the president answered, "The Department of State has issued instructions to its consular officers, which are now in effect, that persons who are obliged to leave the country of their regular residence, and who seek to escape from the conditions of that country by coming to the United States, should receive, on the part of American consular officers, the most considerate attention and the most generous and favorable treatment possible under the laws of this country."[23]

Following the pogroms of November 1938, all Jewish activities in the German economy were prohibited. Jews were forced to live off their savings or receive social assistance from the Jewish congregations. They were drafted into forced labor in factories or had to accept low menial jobs.[24]

Hundreds of Jews appealed for help to the Jewish governor of New York. The Lehman family established a trust fund under the name of "Mayer Lehman Charity Fund" to assist relatives abroad, with Arthur Lehman's daughter, Dorothy Bernhard, in charge. They furnished money for emigration and posted guarantees that the immigrants would not become public charges. At first, the fund and Herbert Lehman also gave affidavits and financial aid to nonrelated refugees. His former secretary, Carolin A. Flexner, remembered one particular incident. When one of Lehman's former partners in the bank refused to give an affidavit to a very distant relative still caught in Nazi Germany, the problem was brought to her attention. She called the governor and told him the situation: "I said, 'Will you give an affidavit for these people? They're going to California. He's an artisan. He'll be on his own. You'll never have anything to do with him, except that it's another family saved.' He said yes."[25] In the late summer of 1939, the Lehmans stopped help to non-relatives because there was no way of handling the numerous requests.[26]

After the pogroms of 1938, the number of immigrants (mostly Jewish) from Germany and Austria, which had been annexed in 1938, rose sharply. In 1938, 17,870 refugees were admitted (65.3 per cent of the quota); in 1939, 27,370 (100 per cent); in 1940, 26,080 (95.3 per cent). In 1941, the year in which emigration from Germany was stopped by the German authorities, the number fell to 13,050 (47.7 per cent). Attempts to introduce legislation in Congress in 1938/39 to permit German-Jewish children to enter outside the quota system failed. A bill to this effect died in committee without reaching the floor of the House of Representatives or the Senate.[27] When Germany closed its doors on October 1, 1941, thousands of Jews who had hoped to emigrate to the United States were caught within Germany's borders. Their names and registration numbers were on long waiting lists. For them the call to the American consulate to undergo the required screening never came.

In March 1940, Governor Lehman received a letter from Lina Neugaß, Berthold's sister. Together with her brother, her brother's wife, and ten other Rieneck Jews she had moved to Frankfurt am Main in 1939; four members of the Jewish community of Rieneck emigrated to Palestine and the United States.[28] "The handwriting and the style are that of a person unused to write letters," Carolin Flexner remarked about the letter when she transcribed it for Herbert Lehman. "Dear Governor: (Lina Neugaß wrote) Please excuse that I approach you. I am unfortunately alone. I have no parents and live here since last year the Jewish community in Rieneck near Gemünden (Main) was dissolved, we all came here. My father was Mendel Neugaß, cattle dealer of Rieneck. I have but one brother, he will soon emigrate, he is married. He got affidavits from his wife's aunt. I live all alone, I am unmarried, forty-nine years old. I always lived with my late parents and helped them. Will you please kindly give affidavits, my registration number is 25,488, but I do not yet have affidavits. I would be most grateful, I hope you won't refuse, please help me and send affidavits, I will then do for you whatever I may be able to do. Unfortunately I have none else to ask. Mrs. Hannchen Stern of Würzburg was my father's cousin. I expect to hear from you very soon and to get affidavits, I would be most thankful."[29] Although the Mayer Lehman Charity Fund tried to help her, Lina Neugaß's emigration proved impossible. At an unknown time, she was deported to an extermination camp in Eastern Europe. No trace remains of her.[30]

Of the estimated 525,000 Jews living in Germany in 1933, between 270,000 and 300,000 succeeded in emigrating, until emigration was officially stopped in 1941. Around 30,000 of those who left Germany were interned in their countries of refuge and perished in the Holocaust, together with those unable to leave.[31]

In the name of the Mayer Lehman Charity Fund, affidavits were signed for ninety people, of whom fifty made it to the United States.[32] Numerous other affidavits were given by individual members of the Lehman family. The fund saw to it that immigrants were picked up at Ellis Island and that lodgings were found for them. The fund paid for social workers who assisted the refugees in financial matters; Governor Lehman and his relatives helped in the search for jobs for the refugees. Often it was Lehman's secretary, Carolin Flexner, or Dorothy Bernhard who kept up contact with the new arrivals and suggested doctors or hospitals when treatment (also paid for by the fund) was necessary.[33]

In four reports on the Charity Fund, Dorothy Bernhard described in full detail the progress of the relatives brought to America. The English of some had improved; others had found better lodgings. A family was given money for buying furniture; the children of an immigrant couple were doing nicely in junior high school. A refugee's bad health did not permit him to work regularly; a young man, although exeedingly intelligent, was emotionally so upset by all he had been through in Germany that he needed psychiatric treatment.[34]

Dorothy Bernhard also informed the readers - relatives who had given money to the Fund - about the successful emigration attempt of another member of the Neugaß family. Max Neugaß, whose great-grandfather, Moses, had been a brother of Isaak Neugaß, had made it to New York via Casablanca and Miami. "Mr. Neugass is forty-four years old (Dorothy Bernhard wrote) and ... he was interned in a concentration camp in Casablanca, which was my reason for giving him an affidavit. Mr. Neugass landed in Miami, Florida, on June 10, 1941. He was detained there by the immigration authorities because he was myoptic and had worn glasses since he was fourteen years old. On this account, the Department of Immigration required the posting of a $500 bond by cash and a report has to be sent in every six months until he becomes a citizen, assuring the immigration officials in Miami that Mr. Neugass has not become a public charge and telling them where he is living. ... Shortly after Mr. Neugass's arrival (in New York) he went to the Employment Department of the National Refugee Service for evaluation. ... In Germany, he was a sales manager for eighteen years in a factory for manufacturing radio parts and screws; therefore he wanted to obtain similar work here. At present, he is employed at the Universal Camera Corporation and is working as a mechanic. ... In September 1941, he sent me a nice appreciative letter and I have heard nothing further from him."[35]

Not all immigrants were able to support themselves. Even in 1957, when Carolin Flexner was interviewed, members of the Lehman family continued to put money into the fund "to keep up the people who are too old to readjust to the life."[36]

96

The Mayer Lehman Charity Fund succeeded in bringing to America at least two grandchildren of Seligmann Lehmann, the fourth Lehmann brother who had stayed in Germany. Mrs. Moses Sinn, her husband, and her daughter, Margot, had secured their visas shortly before July 1, 1941, the day the American consulates in Germany were closed. But it was exeedingly difficult for the fund people to get passages for them at the height of the exodus from Germany. "Their visas would have expired on August 24, 1941, and they sailed from Lisbon on August 20th!" Dorothy Bernhard reported. "The Transmigration Bureau of the Joint Distribution Committee gave invaluable help in keeping constantly on the job concerning the Sinns' transportation. Many cables were sent back and forth and it was a tremendous relief to learn, finally, that they had sailed from Lisbon just in time."[37]

When the Sinn family arrived in New York in September, they were greeted by Mrs. Sinn's cousin, Leo Thalheimer. Leo was the second grandchild of Seligmann Lehmann brought to the United States by the fund. His mother, Eva, and his sister, Lina Hofmann, stayed in Würzburg. Eva Thalheimer, a daughter of Seligmann Lehmann, was eighty-five years old. To be sure, Dorothy Bernhard had signed an affidavit for her, but Eva was unable to get out of Germany. After the U.S. consulates in Germany were closed, emigrants could receive visas only if they succeeded in getting to a neutral country and found a United States consul. For obvious reasons, this was utterly impossible for old Eva Thalheimer. "No one knows what may have happened to these people," Dorothy Bernhard wrote in her fourth report about the family members for whom affidavits had been signed and who were trapped in Europe in the middle of the year 1942.[38]

[1] Herbert H. Lehman, *Reminiscences,* p. 537. Rathenau, a Jew, was killed by right-wing radicals in 1922.

[2] Herbert H. Lehman, *Reminiscences,* p. 538.

[3] Robert Gellately, *The Gestapo and German Society. Enforcing Racial Policy 1933-1945*, Oxford, 1990, pp. 89-90.

[4] Herbert A. Strauss, "Jewish Emigration from Germany. Nazi Policies and Jewish Responses (I)," in *Year Book of the Leo Baeck Institute,* vol. 25, 1980, pp. 330-331.

[5] For a detailed description, cf. Roland Flade, *Der Novemberpogrom von 1938 in Unterfranken. Vorgeschichte, Verlauf, Augenzeugenberichte* (Schriften des Stadtarchivs Würzburg, vol. 6), Würzburg, 1988, pp. 48-59.

[6] Central Archives for the History of the Jewish People, Jerusalem, WR 482 e, pp. 75-76.

[7] Herbert H. Lehman, *Reminiscences,* pp. 538-539.

[8] The most tragic example is Felix Fechenbach, a journalist and politician who grew up in Würzburg and, in 1933, was editor-in-chief of a Detmold Social Democrat newspaper. He was imprisoned in March and killed on August 7, 1933. Roland Flade, "Leben und Tod Felix Fechenbachs," in Felix Fechenbach, *Der Puppenspieler. Ein Roman aus dem alten Würzburg,* ed. by Roland Flade and Barbara Rott, Würzburg, 1988, pp. 25-28.

[9] Gellately, p. 103.

[10] Gellately, p. 108; Strauss, *Jewish Emigration (I),* p. 331.

[11] Flade, *Novemberpogrom,* pp. 72-78.

[12] Baruch Zvi Ophir, Falk Wiesemann (eds.), *Die jüdischen Gemeinden in Bayern 1933-1945. Geschichte und Zerstörung,* München, Wien, 1979. pp. 391-393.

[13] Flade, *Novemberpogrom.* p. 70.

[14] Herbert H. Lehman to Alfred Lewisohn, November 30, 1938 (New York State Archives; New York State Archives Partnership Trust).

[15] Würzburg State Archives, Jüdische Standesregister 110; Gestapostelle Würzburg 8547.

[16] Würzburg State Archives, Gestapostelle Würzburg 8547.

[17] Flade, *Die Würzburger Juden,* pp. 280-281.

[18] Würzburg State Archives, Gestapostelle Würzburg 8547.

[19] Ophir, Wiesemann (eds.), p. 391.

[20] Documents relating to the Mayer Lehman Charity Fund, provided by the Herbert H. Lehman Suite and Papers at Columbia University, New York (letters to Dorothy Bernhard, April 23, 1940; March 7, 1941).

[21] Herbert A. Strauss, "Jewish Emigration from Germany. Nazi Policies and Jewish Responses (II)," in *Year Book of the Leo Baeck Institute,* vol. 26, 1981, pp. 358-359.

[22] Strauss, *Jewish Emigration (II),* p. 361.

[23] Roosevelt's letter is in the custody of the New York State Archives; made available via the New York State Archives Partnership Trust by John L. Loeb, Jr.

[24] Strauss, *Jewish Emigration (I),* p. 332.

[25] Carolin A. Flexner, *Reminiscences,* p. 16; Nevins, p. 199.

[26] Nevins, p. 200.

[27] Strauss, *Jewish Emigration (II),* pp. 359, 362.

[28] Ophir, Wiesemann (eds.), p. 391.

[29] Documents relating to the Mayer Lehman Charity Fund (Herbert H. Lehman Suite and Papers, Columbia University, New York).

[30] Adolf Diamant, *Deportationsbuch der von Frankfurt am Main aus gewaltsam verschickten Juden in den Jahren 1941 bis 1944 (nach den Listen vom Bundesarchiv Koblenz),* Frankfurt, 1984, p. 109.

[31] Strauss, *Jewish Emigration (I),* pp. 326-327.

[32] Dorothy (Mrs. Richard J.) Bernhard, *Fourth Report, Mayer Lehman Charity Fund, June 1, 1941 to June 1, 1942* (Columbia University Libraries, Herbert H. Lehman Suite and Papers).

[33] *Fourth Report,* introduction.

[34] *Fourth Report,* passim.

[35] *Fourth Report,* p. 3.

[36] Carolin A. Flexner, *Reminiscences,* p. 15.

[37] *Fourth Report,* p. 4; the names of Mrs. Sinn's parents are unknown.

[38] *Fourth Report,* pp. 9-10. Apart from Eva Thalheimer and Lina Hofmann, the report listed the following persons still in Germany: Justin Adler with his wife and two children (living in Urspringen near Würzburg), Siegfried Bamberger with his wife (Würzburg), Berthold Hirschberger (Berlin), Selig Koschland with his wife and four children (Haßfurt near Würzburg), Siegfried Lönnerstädter (Haßfurt), Jonas Rosenthal with his wife and three children (Haßfurt), Max Götz with his wife (no place of residence given), and Heinrich Rothschild with his wife (Stuttgart). Günter Böttigheimer, his wife, and his son were living in a camp in unoccupied France; Hugo Bein and Fritz Tannenwald had emigrated to Holland; nothing is known of their fate. Hugo Sichel and his wife had already been deported to a concentration camp in Poland. Seven family members who had been given affidavits had emigrated to Australia, Palestine, and England. *Fourth Report,* passim.

Chapter Twelve

The Ordeal of Eva Thalheimer

Eva Thalheimer was born on April 29, 1856, in Heidingsfeld. She was the third child of Seligmann Lehmann, the fourth Lehmann brother, who had stayed in Germany, and the niece of Henry, Emanuel, and Mayer, who had emigrated to America. When Eva was born, her grandfather Abraham Lehmann was still alive; he saw the girl grow up within the walls of the small medieval town. When he called little Eva, he was reminded of his late wife after whom she had been named. Eva saw her brothers, Benzion and Adolph, and her sister, Hanna, emigrate to the United States. She welcomed Benzion and Hanna back when they returned from Texas.

The synagogue of Veitshöchheim, built between 1727 and 1730 by Schmuhl Moises, great-great-grandfather of Eva Thalheimer's husband Salomon. The interior is dominated by the bimah, where the torah scroll is read. The gallery in the background is reserved for women. (Wolf-Dietrich Weißbach, Würzburg)

Eva Thalheimer and the Lehmans

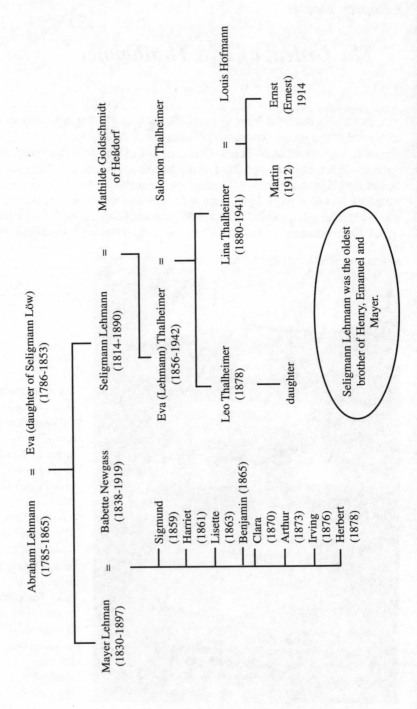

Abraham Lehmann = Eva (daughter of Seligmann Löw)
(1785-1865)   (1786-1853)

Mayer Lehman
(1830-1897)

= Babette Newgass
(1838-1919)

Seligmann Lehmann
(1814-1890)

= Mathilde Goldschmidt
of Heßdorf

Eva (Lehmann) Thalheimer
(1856-1942)

= Salomon Thalheimer

Sigmund
(1859)
Harriet
(1861)
Lisette
(1863)
Benjamin (1865)
Clara
(1870)
Arthur
(1873)
Irving
(1876)
Herbert
(1878)

Leo Thalheimer
(1878)

daughter

Lina Thalheimer
(1880-1941)

= Louis Hofmann

Martin
(1912)

Ernst
(Ernest)
1914

Seligmann Lehmann was the oldest brother of Henry, Emanuel and Mayer.

100

Around 1875, Eva married Salomon Thalheimer, a cattle dealer, and moved to his house on Veitshöchheim's main street, a short distance from the synagogue. Her husband's great-great-grandfather, Schmuhl Moises, had been the man who, with his own money, had built the house of prayer between 1727 and 1730.[1] Today, after having been restored to its original splendor, the temple attracts thousands of visitors every year. Once in a while, members of the small Jewish congregation of Würzburg come to Veitshöchheim to pray in the century-old building.

A son, Leo, was born to Eva and Salomon Thalheimer in 1878. In the 1930s, Leo, by now the owner of a small bank in Würzburg, married and had a daughter.[2] In 1939, the Mayer Lehman Charity Fund helped him and his family emigrate to New York. Leo's sister, Lina, became Lina Hofmann by marrying a Bad Kissingen banker. After Lina's husband had died and her sons Martin and Ernst (Ernest) had gone to the United States, Lina moved in with her mother.[3]

By then, Eva Thalheimer was a widow herself. In the 1920s, the smallish, gray-haired woman had moved to a five-room apartment on Würzburg's Kapuzinerstraße. "She was a high-minded lady," says Mordechai Ansbacher, whose parents and grandparents had long been friends of Eva. Before the Jewish holidays, his parents regularly sent him to Eva Thalheimer with food and freshly baked cakes. "Mrs. Thalheimer was extremely hard of hearing," Mordechai Ansbacher remembers; "She could only communicate with others by using an ear-trumpet."[4]

At 10 A.M. on December 2, 1940, two Gestapo officials searched Eva Thalheimer's apartment. By that time, no German Jew was allowed to have more than one room to himself. That is why three rooms had been sublet to other Würzburg Jews. None of them, however, were present on this morning. Nor was Eva's sixty-year-old daughter Lina, who had been taken to the Jewish hospital because it was suspected that she suffered from cancer. Thus, Eva Thalheimer was all alone in her confrontation with the two Gestapo men who falsely accused her of hoarding clothes and linen. In an internal report, the Gestapo described the visit: "The rooms of (Eva) Thalheimer could not be searched because all wardrobes were locked; the keys are deposited with (her daughter Lina) Hofmann. (Eva) Thalheimer is hard of hearing so that it was almost impossible to talk to her. She was also unable to forward any information on the state of her economic and financial affairs."[5]

Three months later, Eva and her daughter had to move to one of Würzburg's homes for old Jewish people. At this time, damask table-covers, bed clothes, towels, gloves, and two overcoats were confiscated and distributed to non-Jewish families. The two old women were left with the little linen that the Gestapo thought sufficient for somebody who was to be killed very soon anyway. On September 29, 1941, Lina Hofmann died, probably of cancer.[6] No one of Eva's family remained to look after her. Mordechai Ansbacher's mother Minna took over and supported her during the following year.[7]

More and more Jews were forced out of their apartments and crowded together in houses belonging to the Jewish congregation. From 1942, no German Jew was allowed to live in a private house. Even before, Jews had had to turn over their radios, and their telephones had been disconnected. No Jew was permitted on the streets at night; visits to restaurants and public swimming pools were forbidden. The little food Jews were still given had to be bought in particular shops, at particular times. From September 15, 1941, each Jew over six years of age had to wear a yellow star on an outer garment.[8] On November 27, 1941, the first deportation train left Würzburg, carrying 202 Jews from Lower Franconia to a forced labor camp near the Latvian capital, Riga. Among the group were forty boys and girls. Most deportees died in the bitterly cold Latvian winter or were shot within the first weeks.[9] During the next one and a half years, nearly 2,000 more Jews were deported from Lower Franconia to the ghettos and extermination camps of Eastern Europe.[10]

Lower Franconian Jewish deportees, carrying their belongings in bags and bundles, on their way to the Aumühle *freight yard in Würzburg on April 25, 1942. (Ernst Gortner, Nürnberg)*

The news that hundreds of thousands of European Jews were executed by the Germans in areas wrested from the Russians since mid-1941 started to flood the American Jewish press by the summer of 1942. It set off calls for mass protest and American and United Nations action. On July 21, 1942, 20,000 people crowded Madison Square Garden in New York. Among the speakers were Governor Herbert Lehman, Mayor Fiorello La Guardia, a Methodist bishop, and the president of the American Federation of Labor. In a message, President Roosevelt declared that the

American people "will hold the perpetrators of these crimes to strict accountability in a day of reckoning which will surely come."[11]

Eva Thalheimer boarded the train that was never to return on September 23, 1942, together with 561 other persons, among them Minna Ansbacher and her fifteen-year-old son Mordechai. The train's destination was the so-called *Altersghetto* ("ghetto for old people") in Theresienstadt near Prague. Before, Eva had paid 10,400 marks and signed a document *(Heimeinkaufsvertrag)* promising her board and lodging for the rest of her life in a Jewish home.[12] Theresienstadt, however, turned out to be not the "home" many hoped for, but a concentration camp of its own kind.

Mordechai Ansbacher was one of the few survivors among the deportees that left Würzburg on that bleak day in September 1942. Nineteen years later, as witness for the prosecution, he described their ordeal during the Eichmann trial in Jerusalem: "When we were deported, the emporium *(Umschlagplatz)* was the *Platz'scher Garten*, a former theater and coffee-house with large rooms, just what the Gestapo needed. Usually the deportees were brought there one or two days before the train left. Strict regulations were in effect; for example, you were not allowed to go from one room to another. In the 'Large Room' *(Großer Saal)*, it was determined what everybody could take with him. Only the barest necessities were permitted. We were to be transported to Theresienstadt. Everybody was eager to go there, although no one knew exactly what Theresienstadt was. We all had the impression that Theresienstadt would be better than any other place in the East."[13]

Theresienstadt, a former garrison town surrounded by fortifications not unlike those of Würzburg, had been built at the end of the eighteenth century. Fewer than 10,000 people had been living within its walls before the old barracks were turned into lodgings for more than 60,000 Jewish prisoners, many of them old and sick like Eva Thalheimer.[14] "When our Würzburg transport arrived, we were sent to a house carrying the number 11,206," Mordechai Ansbacher said during the Eichmann trial. „Before that, things that we were not allowed to keep were taken away, things like toilet paper, thermos flasks, drinks, and furs. In 11,206, we were given a tiny attic and told: 'Stay here, that is your place.' In the attic I remained for about four weeks; then I was given a place on the floor in a room with old people. One person did not know who was lying besides him; one person did not know who was dying besides him. If I remember correctly, everybody in our little house was from Würzburg. ... We were suffering from terrible hunger; we had no water to wash ourselves. No hygienic precautions whatsoever had been taken. People were dying of hunger and of dysentery. Hungry people fought over potato peelings for a left-over potato."[15]

During September 1942, thirty-eight transports with 18,640 deportees arrived in Theresienstadt. Almost 4,000 people died; 13,000 were removed to extermination camps.[16]

Trapped in an overcrowded attic, without a toilet or water, probably unable to descend the narrow stairs, eighty-six-year-old Eva Thalheimer certainly harbored little hope for a turn to the better. What did she feel when, after a few weeks, she was told that she was to board yet another train? Did she understand? A *Transport* was put together; its destination was Treblinka in the northeast of Warsaw, a new extermination camp whose deadly machinery had started to work three months earlier.[17] This, of course, was a well-kept secret. Eva could not have imagined what was to come.

And so, on an October day in 1942, the last voyage of Eva Thalheimer's long life began,[18] the most tragic of all the many voyages that members of the Lehman family had undertaken since Henry set out for America almost a century earlier. The train headed east, passing through former Czechoslovakia, now the *Reichsprotektorat Böhmen und Mähren*, and through occupied Poland. German troops were fighting thousands of miles further east. Already, they were slowly

"We see a little railroad station with the legend 'Treblinka'" (Yad Vashem, Jerusalem)

retreating under heavy Russian attacks. But mass murder of an unprecedented dimension was to continue for more than two years.

Richard Glazar was twenty-two years old when he stood on the platform in Theresienstadt on October 8, 1942. The train he entered with one thousand others may have been Eva Thalheimer's train. After his liberation, he recorded details of the two days that followed: "The train stops often and, particularly at night, for longer periods. At dawn, after the second night, we see sign-posts and know that we have to be somewhere in Poland. Shortly after noon we stop again. We see a little railroad-station with the legend 'Treblinka.' A part of the train is uncoupled. In a bend we see that the first cars turn unto a single-track railway-line. Forest on both sides. The train moves very slowly. We discern the odd pine, birch-tree, and spruce. The forest clears up; the train passengers come to life, press against the ... windows, but nobody dares look out. High green fence, open gate through which our compartment moves at a leisurely pace. It is 4 P.M., the tenth of October, 1942. 'Get out, everybody get out, faster! Leave your heavy luggage behind, everything will be delivered later!' A ramp, behind it a wooden shack, on the ramp people wearing boots, but in civilian clothes. This one has a long strange-looking club in his hand, a leather whip. Probably ordinary people, no Jews, no one is wearing the yellow star. Between them SS uniforms. also with whips, some with machine-guns.

Looks like a small railroad-station in the Wild West, immediately behind it a farm surrounded by a high green fence. The fence is of a pretty green; it must be a large farm with a lot of cattle .... The new arrivals are directed away from the ramp through another gate to a square. On both sides rows of wooden shacks. 'Men to the right, women with children to the left! Lay down your luggage, undress, undress completely!'"[19]

The naked women and children are led to a *Friseurstube* (*"hairdresser's shop"*) to have their hair cut off. Those who are able to walk have to hand over their documents, watches, and jewelry. Then they are pushed into "shower rooms" and killed by exhaust gas. Sick people and those with difficulty in walking (like, in all probability, Eva Thalheimer) are led to the *Lazarett* ("infirmary"), welcomed by workers with a red cross on their armlet, and shot by an SS man in front of a ditch.[20]

[1] Karen Heußner, Veitshöchheim (letter to the author, September 18, 1995); Karen Heußner, "Jüdisches Kulturmuseum und Synagoge Veitshöchheim. Auf den Spuren einer ehemaligen jüdischen Landgemeinde," in *Schöne Heimat - Erbe und Auftrag. Zeitschrift des Bayerischen Landesvereins für Heimatpflege e.V.*, vol. 97, Munich, 1990.

[2] Würzburg City Archives, Einwohnermeldeamt, Meldebogen Leo Thalheimer; Strätz, *Biographisches Handbuch*, II. Teilband, p. 632.

[3] *Fourth Report*, Section I (B), p. 3; Strätz, *Biographisches Handbuch*, I. Teilband, p. 273; Mordechai Ansbacher, Jerusalem (letter to the author, July 18, 1995).

[4] Mordechai Ansbacher, Jerusalem (letter to the author, July 18, 1995); Nathan Königshöfer, Basel (letter to the author, June 8, 1995).

[5] Würzburg State Archives, Gestapostelle Würzburg 15894.

[6] Würzburg State Archives, Gestapostelle Würzburg 15894; Strätz, *Biographisches Handbuch*, I. Teilband, p. 273.

[7] Mordechai Ansbacher, Jerusalem (letter to the author, July 18, 1995).

[8] Flade, *Würzburger Juden*, pp. 330-331.

[9] Flade, *Würzburger Juden*, pp. 343-354, 362-369.

[10] Flade, *Würzburger Juden*, pp. 354-359.

[11] David S. Wyman, *The Abandonment of the Jews. America and the Holocaust, 1941-1945*, New York, 1984, p. 24.

[12] Würzburg State Archives, Gestapostelle Würzburg 15894.

[13] Dieter W. Rockenmaier, *Das Dritte Reich und Würzburg. Versuch einer Bestandsaufnahme*, Würzburg, 1983, p. 140.

[14] Flade, *Würzburger Juden*, p. 356; Ludmila Chladkova, *Ghetto Theresienstadt*, Terezin, 1991, p. 4.

[15] Flade, *Würzburger Juden*, p. 356.

[16] Hans Günther Adler, *Theresienstadt 1941-1945. Das Antlitz einer Zwangsgemeinschaft. Geschichte, Soziologie, Psychologie*, Tübingen (2nd edition),af 1960, p. 113.

[17] Strätz, II. Teilband, p. 632; Richard Glazar, *Die Falle mit dem grünen Zaun. Überleben in Treblinka*, Frankfurt am Main, 1992, p. 9.

[18] Leo Baeck Institute New York, Kleine Sammlungen, Gemeinde Würzburg, *Würzburger Transport, angekommen Ghetto Theresienstadt 24. 9. 1942*, p. 15.

[19] Glazar, pp. 13-14.

[20] Glazar, pp. 18-20.

Chapter Thirteen

Helping Europeans to Help Themselves

Governor Herbert H. Lehman immediately felt that the United States should be throwing her weight into the balance, when Germany started the Second World War on September 1, 1939.[1] It did, however, take another twenty-seven months until the *Reich* finally declared war on the United States. In the meantime, German forces waged their war of destruction upon large parts of Europe, going along with ruthless economic exploitation and the cold-blooded murder of the Jewish population in country after country.

In the leading circles of the United States, the belief was widespread that help was urgently needed in the war-torn countries. Thus, in November 1942, one year after America's entry into the war, an Office of Foreign Relief and Rehabilitation Operations was created in the State Department. Herbert Lehman, who had decided not to seek a fifth term as governor, became its first director. As he reached the age of sixty-four, a new period in his life began. In the six months of its existence, the Relief office mainly distributed food, medicines, and clothing to the population of North Africa which, by May 1943, had fallen into Allied hands. Camps in the western part of North Africa, filled with refugees from Greece, Yugoslavia, and Poland, also had to be supplied.[2] The relief effort, however, soon proved too much for one nation alone.

On New Year's Day, 1942, twenty-six countries agreed in Washington to form the United Nations, a step that was finally taken in the spring of 1945. Also in 1942, plans for a subsidiary, a United Nations Relief and Rehabilitation Administration (UNRRA), were discussed for the first time. The compact establishing UNRRA was signed by representatives of forty-four nations in a colorful ceremony in the White House on November 9, 1943. Addressing "my friends, on this historic occasion," President Franklin D. Roosevelt, with certain victory of the Allied forces in mind, defined it as UNRRA's task to operate in "areas of food shortage until the resumption of peaceful occupations enables the liberated peoples once more to assume the full burden of their own support. It will be for UNRRA," the president pursued, "first to assume a fair distribution of available supplies among all of the liberated peoples, and, second, to ward off death by starvation or exposure among these peoples." Roosevelt was hopeful as to the future implications of UNRRA's work: "As in most of the difficult and complex things in life, nations will learn to work together only by actually working together," he said.[3]

On November 11, Herbert H. Lehman was elected director general of UNRRA. The organization he headed was to help people to help themselves; it was to distribute its aid without discrimination to all parts of the population in liberated countries. UNRRA was to assist in bringing relief - food, clothing, shelter, and medical supplies

- and rehabilitation. "Rehabilitation" did not mean reconstruction; UNRRA was to provide materials and services required for the resumption of urgently needed agricultural and industrial production and the restoration of essential services. UNRRA was the first large operating international agency. At its peak in June 1946, the UNRRA staff comprised more than 24,000 men and women.[4]

Until relief could be brought to Europe on a large-scale basis, UNRRA had to wait for the progress of the Allied forces. Waiting was painful to Herbert Lehman. In August, 1943, Anglo-American troops had taken possession of Sicily; D Day in Normandy did not come until June 6, 1944. And even when one country after another was liberated, it proved extremely difficult to secure supplies and find transportation, both being desperately needed by the military for a speedy victory. Meanwhile, the liberated zones were being widened and governments in these lands were struggling to shelter the wandering masses of refugees and prisoners, and make urgent provisions of food, clothing, and sanitary supplies for their home populations. "We want desperately to get to work," Lehman said at the time. "But even if we had supplies, we would have no means of getting them into the needy areas of Western Europe unless the military ordered them forward. And the military declines." On December 7, 1944, Lehman appealed to President Roosevelt and asked for the allotment of extra shipping. When the president supported his claim, the military grip upon food, clothing, fuel, and transport was loosened and UNRRA started to fulfil its mission with vigor.

In Italy, mothers and children received supplementary food; medical supplies were delivered, and the miserable situation in refugee camps was improved. Poland, victim of the German strategy of scorched earth, was in most desperate need for almost everything. In March 1945, the first UNRRA shipments were brought through the Rumanian port of Constanza on the Black Sea. In France and Holland, almost one out of five houses had been smashed or burnt. Greece and Yugoslavia were particularly hard hit. Actually, there was almost no place in Europe where help was not needed. On May 8, 1945, Germany surrendered. By June 30, 1945, 1,250,000 tons of UNRRA food, clothing, and other materials had been shipped to Europe. It soon became clear that help had to go mainly to countries in the eastern and the southern sectors of the continent. Belgium, Holland, France, and Norway were able to help themselves.[5]

During a fifty-day journey in the summer of 1945, Herbert Lehman acquainted himself with European problems. In July, when he was brought to the Quirinal Palace in Rome, where children were housed, he had "one of the most affecting and heartbreaking experiences" of his life: "Half of the children are totally blind," he recorded in his diary. "Others have lost one or more limbs. Several of them have terribly lacerated faces. Most of the injuries were sustained from land mines. The children have not yet accustomed themselves to their handicaps. The little blind tots groped around until they found someone to cling to, and then they held my hand in a puzzled, frightened way. The sight was almost more than one could bear." On the Greek island of Crete, he met an old woman in her eighties. "She was almost unable to talk because of her emotion. She told me her only son had been seized by the Germans, who had sprinkled gasoline over him and burned him to death in her presence. I was told that this was only one of thousands of similar incidents. At one place overlooking a ravine, we were told of six hundred patriots who were shot by the Germans and buried in three common graves."[6]

Herbert H. Lehman wishing a safe voyage to Captain McKenzie, Master of the first ship with relief supplies for Poland and Czechoslovakia (Herbert H. Lehman Suite and Papers, Columbia University, New York)

After his return to Washington, it became Lehman's primary concern to secure money for the extraordinary relief effort necessary in Europe. Almost four billion dollars were to be spent by UNRRA until the organization was dissolved in 1947, with most of the money coming from the US, Great Britain, and Canada. The sheer size of UNRRA's programs drew criticism from Americans who thought that their country had done enough for Europe already and that Europeans were now to look after themselves. At a rally in Central Park, Herbert Lehman asked UNRRA's critics: "Are we going to allow starvation in Europe or prevent it? If necessary, are we willing to make a small sacrifice at home in order that millions abroad can regain their health and dignity?" America's answer was "Yes." As part of its rehabilitation program, UNRRA distributed nearly 80,000 trucks and 650 locomotives, badly needed to resume transport of basic goods. Roads, canals, railways, and ports were cleared of debris; mines were reopened and essential industries restarted. Steam-powered electric power stations were built in Byelorussia and the Ukraine.[7]

"In the first half of 1946, the activities of UNRRA were rising toward their height," writes Alan Nevins. "During most of the year, it was the largest exporter in the world. Before the organization ended, it was to deliver to seventeen nations more than 24,000,000 tons of supplies for relief and rehabilitation. ... Supplies were coming in now from all over the globe: coal from South Africa, wheat and wool from Australia, jute from India, sugar from Cuba, fish from Iceland, beans from Peru, lorries from Britain, locomotives from America." At the same time, "UNRRA was conducting the largest international medical program in history, stopping epidemics in their tracks."[8]

In the months following the Allied victory in Europe, millions of captives and refugees choked the highways of the continent: Germans fleeing from the eastern part of the *Reich*, now occupied by the Russians, liberated prisoners of war, former inmates of concentration and extermination camps, many of whom were more dead than alive, foreign workers coerced into German factories and farms on their way home. It was the American military's initial policy to return as many of those displaced persons (DPs) as possible to their countries of origin. Yet many DPs did not want to be repatriated. The majority of the surviving Jews were natives of Eastern Europe; they had no desire to go back to Poland, the Ukraine, or Rumania, countries rampant with anti-Semitism.[9]

In Germany, most displaced persons were housed in former army centers or in wooden barracks which partly had been used as concentration camps or forced labor camps. In July 1945, Earl G. Harrison, dean of the University of Pennsylvania Law School and American member of the Intergovernmental Committee on Refugees, traveled through Germany and Austria. The new American president, Harry S. Truman, had asked him to put together a report on the conditions under which displaced persons, particularly Jewish refugees, were living. Harrison's report was an indictment of military insensitivity to the plight of the Jewish DPs. Many of them, Harrison remarked, "are living under guard behind barbed-wire fences in camps of several descriptions, built by the Germans for slave laborers and Jews, including some of the most notorious concentration camps, amid crowded, frequently unsanitary and generally grim conditions, in complete idleness, with no opportunity, except surreptitiously, to communicate with the outside world, waiting, hoping for some word of encouragement and action on their behalf. ... Although some camp commandants have managed, in spite of the many obvious difficulties, to find clothing of one kind or another for their charges, many of the Jewish displaced persons, late in July, had no clothing other than their concentration camp garb - a rather hideous striped pyjama effect - while others, to their chagrin, were obliged to wear German SS uniforms. ... As matters now stand, we appear to be treating the Jews as the Nazis treated them, except that we do not exterminate them. They are in concentration camps in large numbers under our military guard instead of SS troops." Harrison suggested that the operation of DP camps "should be turned over to a civilian agency - UNRRA."[10]

UNRRA was in charge of most displaced persons in the three western zones of Germany from the fall of 1945; the Russians did not allow the organization to work in its zone of occupation. At the end of 1945, UNRRA supervised 263 assembly centers for displaced persons in Germany alone, plus various others in Austria, Italy, the Middle East, and China. A survey taken in September 1946 listed the following groups under UNRRA care in Germany: 302,000 Poles, many of whom did not want to return to their country with its new Communist government; 176,000 Estonians, Latvians, and Lithuanians, whose home countries had become Soviet Republics; 121,000 Jews, among them survivors of concentration camps, and many postwar refugees from Eastern Europe; 14,000 Yugoslavs; and 81,000 others. The term DP did not embrace the millions of Germans driven out of the Baltic states, Czechoslovakia, Yugoslavia, and former German territories placed under Polish and Russian administration. Although they undoubtedly had been displaced by the war, many of these Germans had been strong supporters of Hitler's war effort. Thus, they were not considered eligible for UNRRA help.[11]

In his report to President Truman, Earl Harrison proposed that the United States should ask Britain to help clear the DP camps by letting 100,000 Jews into Palestine, still administered by the United Kingdom. Harrison also suggested that the United States should accept an equivalent number - much higher than the yearly immigration quota - within its own borders. The London government, however, did not want to inflame Arabs by admitting too many Jews into Palestine. Nor did America relax its immigration laws.[12]

Several DP camps were situated in Lower Franconia, which lay in the U.S. zone of occupation. The largest of all UNRRA camps, with over 15,000 inhabitants, was established in Wildflecken in the Rhön Mountains.[13] Displaced persons were also living in Würzburg, Aschaffenburg, Seligenstadt, Lohr, Kleinheubach, and Schweinfurt.[14] Würzburg, destroyed almost completely by the Royal Air Force during a bomb attack on March 16, 1945, housed up to 5,000 DPs, mostly Latvians, in various barracks compounds. By 1949, the number had fallen to 3,700. German police were barred entry to the camps.[15] From 1945 to 1949, more than 1,200 Lithuanians were living in a former *Wehrmacht* camp in Seligenstadt, a few miles from Würzburg. Some of them returned to the little village in 1993 when Kazimiera Prunskiene, who had been the first prime minister of Lithuania after its independence from the Soviet Union, visited Seligenstadt.[16] In 1947, a camp was opened in Giebelstadt, near Würzburg, for 2,000 Jewish DPs. Most of them emigrated to Israel, the United States, and Canada two years later. Some joined the new Jewish community of Würzburg which had been founded by a few Holocaust survivors.[17]

UNRRA introduced self-government in all camps. Police and fire departments were organized. Primary and secondary schools were opened, with UNRRA providing teachers and educational material. Many camps had vocational training

110

courses. On February 16, 1946, UNRRA established its own university in Munich. One hundred forty-two Jews were among the 2,174 students attending lectures and courses. In May 1947, the institution closed its doors. Students who did not emigrate finished their education at the Bavarian universities of Munich, Erlangen, and Würzburg.[18]

Zionism gained a strong foothold among Jewish DPs in Germany. In the autumn of 1945, David Ben-Gurion, then chairman of the Jewish Agency, addressed a huge crowd of displaced persons in the Bavarian town of Landsberg. "A Jewish power has arisen which will fight together with you for a proud, independent Palestine," he said. "I promise you that not only your children but also we, the white-haired ones, will live to see the Jewish homeland." A great number of DPs emigrated illegally to Palestine. On May 14, 1948, Ben-Gurion read the Declaration of Independence of the State of Israel.[19] For many years, he was Israel's prime minister.

Herbert Lehman resigned as director general of UNRRA on March 12, 1946. He was approaching his sixty-eighth birthday and felt exhausted. He had the impression that President Truman was not the ardent supporter of UNRRA's work that Franklin Roosevelt had been. Also, criticism of the organization's alleged deficiencies (too much red tape, unqualified personnel) worried Lehman. His successor as director general was Fiorello La Guardia, longtime mayor of New York.[20]

[1] Nevins, pp. 209, 222.

[2] Nevins, pp. 222, 227.

[3] George Woodbridge, *UNRRA: The History of the United Nations Relief and Rehabilitation Administration*, New York, 1950, vol I, p. 4; Nevins, p. 224.

[4] Woodbridge, vol. I, pp. 29-30, 149, 244; Woodbridge, vol II, p. 535.

[5] Nevins, pp. 255-268.

[6] Nevins, pp. 264-265. Lehman had also lost a child during the war. His son, Peter, a member of the Army Air Corps, was killed in a flying accident in March 1944, leaving a widow, Peggy, and two girls, Penelope (born in 1940) and Wendy (1942); Nevins, p. 243; Genealogical Record of the Mayer Lehman Family.

[7] Nevins, pp. 270, 276, 281-284.

[8] Nevins, pp. 286-287.

[9] Howard M. Sachar, *A History of Israel. From the Rise of Zionism to Our Time*, New York, 1979, p. 249; Nevins, p. 263.

[10] Juliane Wetzel, *Jüdisches Leben in München, 1945-1951. Durchgangsstation oder Wiederaufbau?* (Miscellanea Bavarica Monacensia, vol. 135), München, 1987, Quellenanhang, no page; Woodbridge, vol. II, p. 500. As late as November 1945, a committee representing the 15,000 residents of the DP camp in Wildflecken (Lower Franconia) complained that "our camp is occupied more rigorously than were concentration camps during the war or German cities since the peace." Leonard Dinnerstein, *America and the Survivors of the Holocaust*, New York, 1982, p. 15.

[11] Woodbridge, vol. II, pp. 485-500.

[12] Wetzel, Quellenanhang; Sachar, p. 256; Nevins, p. 295.

[13] Woodbridge, vol. II, pp. 501-502.

[14] Wetzel, Quellenanhang.

[15] Herbert Schott, *Die Amerikaner als Besatzungsmacht in Würzburg, 1945-1949* (Mainfränkische Studien, vol. 33), Würzburg, 1985, pp. 73-74.

[16] Tilman Toepfer, "Den litauischen Reiter enthüllt," in *Main-Post*, Würzburg, January 9, 1993.

[17] Flade, *Würzburger Juden*, p. 389. In 1970, a new synagogue was opened in Würzburg. In 1995, around 300 Jews were living in Lower Franconia, compared to 9,000 in 1933. Of more than 100 Jewish congregations in the governmental district that perished during the Holocaust, only the one in Würzburg was reestablished. One out of three Jewish citizens of today's Lower Franconia is a former citizen of the U.S.S.R.

[18] Bernhard Zittel, "Die UNRRA-Universität in München 1945-1947," in *Archivalische Zeitschrift*, vol. 75, 1979, p. 286; Wetzel, p. 124.

[19] Sachar, pp. 261, 311.

[20] Nevins, pp. 296-299.

Epilogue

Herbert H. Lehman's period of rest did not last long. In the fall of 1946, he was on the campaign trail again, running for a senatorial seat. 1946, however, was a year in which Lehman's ideas of a higher minimum wage and a national health program were not popular. All over the country, the Republicans triumphed in the elections and Lehman was defeated. Three years later, when a New York Senate seat became vacant, the seventy-one-year-old former governor ran again; this time he beat John Foster Dulles. By now, Lehman had become the leading Jewish figure in public life, known for his support of liberal causes and the State of Israel.[1] As with all the jobs he took on, Lehman prepared thoroughly for his senatorial duties, with eight fulltime research workers backing him up. Among the friends Lehman made in the Senate were such liberal Democrats as Hubert Humphrey of Minnesota, Wayne Morse of Oregon, and Henry M. Jackson of Washington. Together with other New Dealers,

Shortly after Senator John F. Kennedy had declared his run for the President of the United States, he met Herbert H. Lehman in the Beverly Wilshire Hotel in Beverly Hills on July 15, 1960. (Herbert H. Lehman Suite and Papers, Columbia University, New York)

these men witnessed major proposals of President Truman, like national health insurance and civil rights legislation, blocked by a coalition of Republicans and conservative Democrats.

As the profits of companies selling material for the Korean War effort exploded, Lehman fought for a higher taxation of these firms. On June 7, 1951, he delivered a rousing speech on the subject: "While the reactionary elements in Congress slash away at funds for public health, public power, and public housing - under the guise of economy - they move very slowly, indeed, to tax the unprecedented profits of big business. In the second half of 1950, American corporations made an average of 17.5 percent profit, after taxes, on the investment of their stockholders. In one of the largest industries these profits, for the last quarter of 1950, after taxes, amounted to 25 per cent. But no new taxes have yet been enacted to tap these profits, made possible by the defense effort."[2]

There can be no doubt as to Herbert H. Lehman's greatest achievement in politics: his year-long fight against Senator Joseph McCarthy, whose anti-Communist witch-hunt was poisoning the political climate of the nation. Time and again, Lehman stood up on the Senate floor to expose McCarthy's falsehoods and character assassinations. He attacked him on radio, on televison, and during the meetings of a hundred organizations, until McCarthy's downfall came in 1954.[3]

Among the causes Lehman fought for most fervently as a senator were the civil rights of the black population. During the 1956 presidential race, he tried in vain to insert a strong civil-rights plank into the platform of the Democrats. The franchise could no longer be denied any group, he declared. Authority had to be given to the attorney general to enforce penalties when black citizens were deprived of their Constitutional rights. Lehman failed. He was also unsuccessful when, together with other Senate liberals, he demanded a compulsory program that would end poll taxes, intimidation of black voters, and racial discrimination in employment and transportation. It was failures like these, combined with the fact that he was seventy-eight years old now, that contributed to Lehman's decision not to run again in 1956. "No one can look back with greater satisfaction than you can on a life of public service," Eleanor Roosevelt wrote to her close friend after he had left the Senate.[4]

Herbert Lehman had seven more years still before him and he remained active. In 1960, when the Democrats decided on their presidential candidate, he strongly supported Adlai Stevenson, who had been defeated by Dwight D. Eisenhower twice. But after John F. Kennedy was nominated, Lehman gave him vigorous support and made more than twenty addresses for him.[5]

Herbert H. Lehman died on December 5, 1963, two weeks after John F. Kennedy had been shot and killed in Dallas. Lehman's memory is kept alive by Allan Nevins's biography *Herbert H. Lehman and His Era*, published shortly before Lehman's death. Columbia University houses the Herbert H. Lehman Suite and Papers, where the governor's personal and official papers, as well as fourteen related collections, are kept.[6]

Lehman Brothers, the firm that his father and uncles founded, today is one of

The Lehman Wing of the Metropolitan Museum of Art in New York (Metropolitan Museum of Art, New York)

the leading global investment banks. In 1993, the bank had approximately 9,000 employees in thirty-five offices around the world, among them Frankfurt and Hamburg. As successor to Emanuel and Mayer Lehman and to Philip Lehman in the role of major partners, Philip's son Robert began to assume the principal responsibilities about 1925 when he was only thirty-four years old. He led the firm until his death in 1969. In 1963, General Lucius D. Clay joined Lehman Brothers as one of four senior partners. He had been commander of the United States forces in Europe following World War II and leader of the Berlin airlift. Around 1980, Lehman Brothers merged with Kuhn, Loeb & Co. which, under the direction of Jacob Schiff (1847-1920), had become one of the world's foremost financial institutions. Shortly after the merger, in 1984, Lehman Brothers ceased to be a private partnership and was taken over by American Express. Only one family member, Philip Isles, the great-grandson of Emanuel Lehman, remained with Shearson Lehman Hutton, as the new firm was called. In 1994, Lehman Brothers became independent again.[7]

Robert Lehman, longtime head of Lehman Brothers, was also a major art collector. The collection was originally started by his father, Philip Lehman, and exhibited in the latter's New York house on West 54th Street. Robert added so enormously to it that it became the largest, and possibly the finest, in America. He brought together paintings and drawings of artists like Botticelli, Rembrandt, El Greco, Goya, Renoir, van Gogh, Leonardo da Vinci, Degas, and Cézanne. The

Robert Lehman Collection also includes magnificent examples of the decorative arts: Gothic tapestries and embroideries, medieval bronze aquamanilia, Renaissance bronzes and medals, Venetian glass, and superb goldsmith's work and jewelry. When Robert Lehman died in 1969, he donated some 3,000 works of art to the Metropolitan Museum in New York under the condition that they were to be shown in a new annex. The Lehman Wing, comprising a series of period rooms, duplicated from the old Lehman home on West 54th Street, and galleries built around a garden court, was opened in 1975.[8]

It was in the Lehman Wing of the Metropolitan Museum of Art where, on June 15, 1989, some 170 members of the Lehman family congregated for a family reunion. Wendy Lehman Lash, a granddaughter of Governor Lehman, had taken the initiative in bringing the clan together and had organized the party with John L. Loeb, Jr., a great-great-grandson of Abraham Lehmann and a former U.S. ambassador to Denmark.[9] Chamber music played in the background while four generations of Lehmans gathered around a huge family tree displayed on a wall, still unframed in case anybody's name was spelled wrong.[10]

At the bottom of the tree, where the roots were thickest, was the name of the man who, two centuries earlier, had held a letter of protection in his hand.

---

[1] In 1955, Lehman donated to the Israeli desert town of Dimona a school that was named after his wife. Today, students from the Edith Lehman High School meet regularly with students from Würzburg's Wirsberg-Gymnasium. Ilona Hoppmann, "Partnerschaft mit der Edith-Lehman-Schule," in *Main-Post*, Würzburg, April 4, 1995.

[2] Nevins, pp. 303-325. Lehman was reelected to the Senate during the regular elections of 1950; Nevins, p. 329.

[3] Birmingham, pp. 337-338; Nevins, p. 346.

[4] Nevins, pp. 364-367, 370.

[5] Nevins, pp. 382-383.

[6] *The Herbert H. Lehman Suite and Papers at Columbia University* (folder).

[7] *Centennial*, pp. 39-40; *Lehman Brothers. The Tradition Continues,* New York, 1994, passim; "Lehman Brothers wird selbständig," in *Börsen-Zeitung*, April 7, 1994; "American Express trennt sich von Lehman Brothers," in *Süddeutsche Zeitung*, January 26, 1994.

[8] Howard Hibbard, *The Metropolitan Museum of Art, New York*, London, Boston, 1980, p. 574; Birmingham, p. 380; *Michelin Tourist Guide, New York City*, New York, 1979, pp. 57-58. Robert Lehman's collection also comprises various drawings by Giovanni Battista Tiepolo, a Venetian painter who, between 1752 and 1753, created a monumental fresco for the Great Staircase of the Würzburg *Residenz*. When an exhibition commemorating the 300th birthday of Tiepolo was shown in the *Residenz* in the spring of 1996, several drawings by Tiepolo and his son Giovanni Domenico were on loan from the Lehman Collection of the Metropolitan Museum. Peter O. Krückmann (ed.), *Der Himmel auf Erden. Tiepolo in Würzburg,* vol. 1, München, 1996, pp. 96, 187.

[9] John L. Loeb, Jr., received a bachelor's degree cum laude from Harvard College and a master's degree in business administration from the Harvard Business School. He served as a first lieutenant in the U.S. Air Force. He became a partner in Loeb, Rhoades in 1959 and was the firm's president from 1971 to 1973. Loeb served as special advisor on environmental matters to New York Governor Nelson A. Rockefeller from 1967 to 1973. From 1981 to 1983, he was U.S. ambassador to Denmark. In late 1983, he served as a U.S. representative to the General Assembly of the United Nations. Loeb is now

chairman of John L. Loeb, Jr., Associates, an investment counseling firm in New York. His sister, Ann, was married to Edgar M. Bronfman, president of Seagrams and president of the World Jewish Congress. John L. Loeb, Jr., is president of the Winston Churchill Foundation of the United States, which supports a scholarship and fellowship program under which American graduate students and professors attend Churchill College at Cambridge University for advance work in science and technology. Nadine Brozan, "Chronicle," in the *New York Times*, December 23, 1994; *The International Who's Who, 1991-1992*, 55th edition, London, 1991, pp. 992-993.

[10] Georgia Dullea, "Lehman Wingding in Lehman Wing," in the *New York Times,* June 16, 1989.

Postscript

Rimpar, June 1996

It was a warm and bright June morning in 1996. Ruth Thalheimer Nelkin was having breakfast in her Great Neck, N.Y. home, when an article in the newspaper caught her eye. It told about the forthcoming reunion of members of the Lehman family in Würzburg and of a ceremony in a small nearby town. Though the name of Rimpar meant nothing to her, Würzburg did. It was the city where she had been born in 1937. The name Lehman brought back memories from a time that had been anything but warm and bright: of her grandmother, Eva Thalheimer, who had been killed in Treblinka; of her parents, Leo and Selma Thalheimer, with whom she had to emigrate from Nazi Germany when she was only two; of her father who, after *Kristallnacht,* was held captive in the Buchenwald concentration camp and later, in the United States, would refuse to talk about his experiences.

There were fond memories, too. Of Herbert H. Lehman, the New York governor, who had not just saved Ruth and her parents by sending an affidavit, but had invited them to Thanksgiving dinners after they had settled down in the United States. The governor and the Mayer Lehman Charity Fund continued to care for the Thalheimer family, as they did for so many others. "He sent my father a hundred and twenty-five dollars every month, and when my father died he sent the check to my mother," Ruth Nelkin remembers. "I think the checks would still be coming if I hadn't called to tell them when my mother had died. They asked me if I still needed help, and I didn't."[1]

Over the years, Ruth Nelkin, a stockbroker, had lost contact with her relatives. Now she read that the story of the Lehmans' emigration to the United States and the ordeal of her grandmother, Eva Thalheimer, had been documented, that a permanent exhibition was to be opened in Rimpar castle, and that the mayor of Rimpar, Anton Kütt, had invited the family to a ceremony. She called the newspaper and was informed that the man behind the reunion was John L. Loeb, Jr., the retired United States ambassador to Denmark. However, he had already left for Europe.

During a stopover in London, John Loeb heard of Ruth Nelkin's message and returned her call. He had known that Leo Thalheimer had a daughter but had no idea how to reach her. On the spot, he invited her to join the group. She left things open for the moment. She had never been back to Germany. Also, her husband strongly advised against any trip to the land of the Holocaust.

Two days later, on Thursday, June 14, Ambassador Loeb called again, this time from Würzburg. He told Ruth Nelkin that there was still room for her if she wanted to come. Still she did not say "yes," but she could not stop thinking about the trip. "I woke up in the middle of the night knowing I had to go or I'd regret it the rest of my life," she later described the moment when she made her decision. "It was 4 a.m. when I woke my husband and told him. I called John Loeb in Germany, where it was 10 a.m., and I started packing."

At 7 a.m., Ruth Nelkin phoned her son and daughter. "I said, 'Auf Wiedersehn,' and asked them to join me." Her son Leslie could not make it, but her daughter, Amy, an attorney, was able to make arrangements at work and to join her mother's odyssey. The two left New York on Friday, June 15. In Würzburg and Rimpar they were to meet relatives whom they had never seen before and whose very existence was new to them. These relatives, too, had had no idea that Eva Thalheimer's granddaughter had been living on Long Island for decades.

Eva Thalheimer in the 1930s. The man shown on her pin is probably her husband Salomon Thalheimer, who had died in 1900 at the age of 50. (Ruth Thalheimer Nelkin, Great Neck, N.Y.)

Ruth Nelkin took with her old photographs and documents that were to shed new light on the history of the Lehman family.[2] Most importantly, she brought a photograph of Eva Thalheimer. Until then, no one in the family knew how she had looked.

In Würzburg, meanwhile, descendants of Mayer and Emanuel Lehman were arriving from the United States and Great Britain for the reunion. Among them were Lord William Goodhart[3] of London, a vice-chairman of the Human Rights Institute of the International Bar Association and a co-founder of the Liberal

Democratic Party of Great Britain, his wife, Celia, Lady Goodhart, his daughter Laura, a journalist, and his nephew David Goodhart,[4] editor-in-chief of the London-based current affairs monthly, *Prospect*.

From New York came Wendy Lehman Lash,[5] a civic leader, composer William Mayer,[6] Terry Asiel,[7] a psychiatric social worker, and William Bernhard, a foundation executive.[8] From elsewhere in the United States arrived Cynthia Rubinfien,[9] a writer for the *Philadelphia Inquirer*, Charles Chiara,[10] a Hollywood

In the Jewish cemetery of Heidingsfeld, Ambassador John L. Loeb, Jr. laid a stone on Benzion (Zion M.) Lehmann's gravestone. Onlookers were (from left) Ruth Thalheimer Nelkin, Charles Chiara with one-year-old son Julian, and David Schuster, president of the Jewish congregation of Würzburg. (Norbert Schwarzott, Main-Post, Würzburg)

filmmaker, Richard N. Beaty, Jr.,[11] a director of the Dianetic Center of New Jersey, and Orin McCluskey,[12] an investment manager and attorney.[13]

That this was not just any family get-together was made abundantly clear by the messages waiting for the Lehmans upon their arrival in Würzburg. In a letter from the White House, President Bill Clinton wrote: "Distinguishing themselves as public servants, financiers, humanitarians, and upstanding citizens, members of the Lehman family have contributed much to America's success and have brought

Martina Edelmann of the village of Veitshöchheim (left) is explaining to Ruth Nelkin a family tree which traces the roots of her family back to the eighteenth century. Onlookers are John L. Loeb, Jr. (second from left) and Stephen Lash, vice chairman of the auction house, Christie's. (Wolf-Dietrich Weißbach, Würzburg)

honor to their name and to the city of Rimpar. Germans and Americans alike are proud to claim this family as their own, and their ongoing success is a testament to the spirit and values of both our nations."[14]

German chancellor Helmut Kohl wrote of a unique event. By accepting the invitation from Rimpar, the members of the Lehman family had shown their appreciation of the decision of Rimpar's municipal council to keep alive, right in the center of the village, the memory of Jewish life in Rimpar and of the victims of the Holocaust.

In a personal message, New York Governor George E. Pataki offered "greetings and congratulations as the light of public recognition shines brightly upon the Lehman family and its descendants." Among the letters received by the family was also one from Dr. Ronald B. Sobel, Senior Rabbi at Congregation Emanu-El in New York City. "The Lehman name stands prominent on the topography of American life and the landscape of twentieth century Jewish history," he wrote, mentioning Mayer, Emanuel, and Irving, and Herbert Lehman's

The Lehman delegation in the park of Veitshöchheim, which surrounds yet another residence of the prince-bishops of Würzburg. (Wolf-Dietrich Weißbach, Würzburg)

work for the congregation and Jewish philanthropic agencies. "Today, the Lehman tradition continues at Temple Emanu-El, as Robert M. Morgenthau and Robert A. Bernhard[15] serve on the Temple's Board of Trustees," the rabbi added, specifically mentioning also the father of John L. Loeb, Jr.,[16] John L. Loeb, Sr., who had spent many years on the Temple board.

The three-day program upon which Ruth Nelkin and the other Lehmans embarked on Saturday, June 15, included a visit to the Jewish cemetery of Heidingsfeld, where John L. Loeb, Jr., placed a stone on the gravestone of his ancestor Benzion (Zion M.) Lehmann, brother of Eva Thalheimer. The group also saw the graves of Joseph Rosenheim, brother of Eva Lehmann, and of Babette Newgass's parents, Isaak and Friederike Neugaß.

In neighboring Veitshöchheim, the delegation was shown the newly restored synagogue, built more than two and a half centuries earlier by the Thalheimer family, who lived in the community. With her daughter Amy, Ruth Nelkin had a highly emotional stroll through Würzburg's Kapuzinerstraße to the house where she was born and had lived with her parents until the family's emigration.

Walking through the street where she spent the first two years of her life brought back memories of another street in Brooklyn, where the family had settled after it arrived in the United States. Her mother found some domestic work, baby-

122

sitting, and cleaning a synagogue, but her father, Leo Thalheimer, by then sixty-four years old, never found work. Ruth quickly became Americanized, and began going to the movies on Saturday afternoons, which bothered her Orthodox father.[17]

Among the many family documents that Ruth Nelkin has preserved is the affidavit given by Herbert Lehman's brother, Arthur, to her cousin Ernest (Ernst) Hofmann. The letter sent to the American consulate in Stuttgart, Germany, contains the famous LPC [likely to become a public charge] clause: "I feel confident that he (Ernest Hofmann) will make a desirable resident of these United States and that he will be able to maintain himself in this country (Arthur Lehman wrote). In order that there may be no question about this point I will undertake to see that, if admitted to this country, he does not become a public charge." Because of this simple letter, Ernest was saved, as were so many others, about whom similar letters were written.

In Würzburg, John L. Loeb, Jr. attended a Sabbath service in the synagogue and talked to members of the congregation, some of whom, upon his invitation, came to the Rimpar ceremony a few days later. He learned about the current influx of Jewish immigrants from the former Soviet Union and the congregation's financial problems caused by large efforts to provide religious education for hundreds of new members who had grown up in an atheist country and had been denied any knowledge of Judaism.

In Rimpar, a plaque was unveiled at the former house of Abraham Lehmann, which is now a pharmacy, and a permanent exhibition was opened in a room of

The old Lehman building on Niederhoferstraße in Rimpar now houses a pharmacy. (Roland Flade, Würzburg)

Rimpar castle, now used as the town hall. At the opening ceremony, Dr. Wolfgang Bötsch, German Minister for Telecommunication, spoke about emigrants like the Lehmans as having shaped America's economics, culture, and politics, helping to build a "transatlantic bridge" that had carried Germany "in numerous important moments of our history."[18]

John Loeb, on behalf of the Lehman family, first thanked the members of the municipal council of Rimpar for their decision to fund the exhibition project, then he thanked Christian Will, a former member of the Bavarian parliament, for meeting the costs of the plaque. He called it "a mark of the spirit now alive in Germany that the home of an unknown Jewish resident of Rimpar, Abraham Lehmann, who lived here some two hundred years ago, should be given landmark status and that the history of the Jewish community of Rimpar, and the fate of its members who were victims of the Holocaust, should be memorialized in your beautiful town hall."

After the opening of the permanent exhibition in Rimpar castle (from right to left): Dr. Wolfgang Bötsch, German Minister for Telecommunications, John L. Loeb, Jr., Lord William Goodhart, David Goodhart, and Christian Will. (Wolf-Dietrich Weißbach, Würzburg)

The exhibition tells the stories of the Lehmans and of Rimpar's Jewish citizens, emphasizing common traits such as loyalty to family and country. Four Rimpar Jews died for their fatherland in World War I. At the same time, Rimpar's Jewish doctor was responsible for the military hospital in the village. Today, visitors of the exhibition on the ground floor of the town hall also learn about the twelve Rimpar Jews who were killed during the Holocaust.[19]

Ambassador John L. Loeb, Jr., and Ignatz Bubis (right), president of the Central Council of Jews in Germany, after the latter's speech in the Knights' Hall. Seated (from left): Ruth Nelkin and Orin McCluskey. (Wolf-Dietrich Weißbach, Würzburg)

As representatives of the Lehman family and of Rimpar's Jewish community, Herbert H. Lehman, governor and senator, and Julie Lassmann, daughter of Rimpar's cantor, play central roles in the exhibition. The two never met, but they were driven by the same urge to help. Julie Lassmann, a licensed language teacher born in 1905, did not emigrate during the Third Reich, probably because her old parents needed her. Julie taught piano to Rimpar boys and girls, both Jewish and non-Jewish, sang traditional Franconian songs with them, and staged small theatrical productions. Julie was also the organizer of cultural events for the Jewish congregation, a writer, a poet, and an inspiration to a generation of Jewish children and adults in Rimpar.[20]

Around 1935, Julie Lassmann went to Würzburg where she worked as a language teacher for the Jewish community. Knowing how to speak English and French did not save her, however. Those were not the languages spoken in Auschwitz to which, together with the last remaining Lower Franconian Jews, she was deported on June 17, 1943.[21]

Julie Lassmann's name was mentioned several times during the main ceremony of the family reunion that took place in the Knights' Hall of Rimpar castle on Monday, June 17, 1996. The room was packed to capacity, with many young faces in the crowd. They belonged to students from Würzburg's Wirsberg-

Lord Goodhart during his address in the Knight's Hall. Standing to his right is translator Gunter Schönweitz, teacher at the Würzburg Wirsberg-Gymnasium.

Gymnasium, sister school of the Edith Lehman High School in Dimona, Israel,[22] and to students from Rimpar's Matthias-Ehrenfried-Schule and Maximilian-Kolbe-Schule.

Among the guests of honor was Duke Max of Bavaria, whose forefathers, at a time when the Lehmans still lived in Rimpar, had been kings of Bavaria. From Lehman Brothers' Frankfurt office, two leading representatives, Frank Beelitz and Dr. Peter Coym, had come. Also in attendance were Ignatz Bubis, president of the Central Council of Jews in Germany, Agota Kuperman, cultural attaché at the American Embassy in Bonn, and David Schuster, president of the Jewish congregation of Würzburg.

During the ceremony, much was said about the past, although Germany's present was not forgotten. "Germans incurred a burden of guilt beyond measure," Herman Leeb, Bavarian Minister of Justice, said. "Even today, we have to face this fact. The uniqueness of the crimes perpetrated by the National Socialists, and of the

Holocaust in particular, shall never be forgotten, suppressed or concealed." Leeb mentioned "Germany's special obligation to stand up to any attempt at reducing German guilt through offsetting." Citing occurrences of burning synagogues, desecrated Jewish cemeteries, and attacks on the homes of foreigners and asylum seekers, Leeb spoke of "assaults on our democratic culture," the perpetrators of which were being persecuted and punished with the full force of the law.

John L. Loeb, Jr., in conversation with Dr. Peter Coym and Frank Beelitz, two leading representatives of Lehman Brothers' Frankfurt office.

During the moving ceremony, lines from Yehuda Amichai, a famous Israeli poet born in Würzburg, were quoted. "The worst has happened and nobody must ever forget it. There are two peoples who must not forget it, the Germans and the Jewish people. To forget is human and also inhuman. We want to forget and have to remember. We want to remember and have to forget. To us all, this is a matter of survival and of healing. The scar, even if it does not hurt any more, warns us of the worst. But at the same time, a scar means also healing and further growth."[23]

The event had a profound effect also on composer William Mayer. He said that he "had always thought of the Lehman family as charmed and protected from the misfortunes that befell so many other Jewish families." After his return to New York, he wrote: "The account of Eva Thalheimer exploded that myth, as did the

Duke Max of Bavaria, whose forefathers had been kings of Bavaria, in conversation with Karin Beaty (center) and the Chiara family after the ceremony in the Knights' Hall. In the background (from left): Stephen Lash, Wendy Lehman Lash (with back to camera), and John L. Loeb, Jr. (Wolf-Dietrich Weißbach, Würzburg)

reference to other family members whom Herbert Lehman could not save. I had always thought of the Holocaust as some remote horror that I was looking down at from a safe distance away. But for the forced journey of the younger Lehman brothers to another country, I might well have been a Holocaust victim, along with so many others."[24]

The Rimpar ceremony was widely reported in the international press. Articles appeared, among others, in the *Daily Telegraph* (London),[25] the *Financial Times* (London),[26] the *New York Post,*[27] the *International Herald Tribune,*[28] the *New York Times,*[29] and the *Süddeutsche Zeitung* (Munich).[30]

In an article published in numerous American-Jewish periodicals during the weeks that followed the Lehman family's journey to Rimpar, Ambassador Loeb talked about his feelings at the event. "As the ceremonies proceeded, I felt a flood of emotions," he wrote. "I thought of my mother, how proud she had been of her family and their record of accomplishment. There are no Jews in Rimpar today. How moving, how ironic, how strange, this whole occasion. The citizens of Rimpar were honoring a Jewish family that was unknown to them until today. Members of the Rimpar municipal council had voted unanimously to fund this project. The chancellor of Germany was writing us; our relatives buried in the lovely Jewish cemetery of Heidingsfeld, now part of Würzburg, rest in immaculately tended grounds. As I listened to the words of praise, of regret, of warning, I thought how much fate and circumstance played in our lives and how lucky I was that my great-grandfather had the good sense and the ambition to emigrate to the United States."[31]

[1] Betty Rosenzweig, "The Lehmans Return to Germany," in *Great Neck Record,* July 18, 1996.

[2] Among the material were letters written in German by Emanuel Lehman between 1898 and 1904 to his brother Seligmann's widow, Mathilde, in Heidingsfeld, and Mathilde's daughter, Eva Thalheimer, in Veitshöchheim. Each letter contained a considerable sum of money given by Emanuel and his sister-in-law, Babette Lehman. Both Emanuel and Babette were living in New York at the time. Emanuel showed great interest in the goings-on in Germany. On May 12, 1903, he asked Eva Thalheimer when the marriage of her daughter Lina to Bad Kissingen banker Louis Hofmann would take place, signing the letter, "Your devoted uncle Emanuel." When Emanuel died in 1907, Lehman Brothers continued to forward money on a regular basis. In 1925, it was Herbert Lehman who personally saw to it that money was sent. In a letter to Leo Thalheimer dated October 13, 1925, and written in perfect German as well, he also promised to send worn clothes, something that he obviously had done before. Letters provided by Ruth Thalheimer Nelkin, Great Neck, NY.

[3] Lord William Goodhart, a grandson of Hattie Lehman and Philip Goodhart, has had a distinguished international career in both law and politics. He was called to the Bar in 1957, appointed Queen's Counsel in 1979, and, from 1975 to 1995, served as Head of Chambers. A graduate from Cambridge University with First Class Honors and a Master of Law from Harvard University, he is a member of the executive committee of the International Commission of Jurists and a vice-chairman of the Liberal Democrat Policy Committee. His work has been published extensively in both the legal and the political arenas. Lord Goodhart was knighted for political and public service in 1989 and was made a life peer by Queen Elizabeth II in 1997. Lord William Goodhart's brother, Charles, is a professor at the London School of Economics and now serves on the Interest Rate Committee of the Bank of England.

[4] David Goodhart, the son of Sir Philip Goodhart, is a graduate of York University. Before founding *Prospect,* he worked for twelve years as a journalist on the *Financial Times,* including three years, from 1988 to 1991, in Germany. Sir Philip Goodhart is a brother of Lord Goodhart. For over 30 years, he was a Conservative member of the House of Commons.

[5] Wendy Lehman Lash is a daughter of Herbert Lehman's son Peter. Her husband, Stephen Lash, also present in Würzburg and Rimpar, is a vice chairman of the auction house, Christie's, Inc. Wendy Lehman Lash compiled *The Lehman Family Directory,* published in 1995. As mentioned above, she was the prime mover in organizing the Lehman family reunion in the Lehman Wing of the Metropolitan Museum of Art in 1989.

[6] William Mayer, the composer, is a grandson of Jules Ehrich and Emanuel Lehman's daughter Evelyn. His works have been performed around the world. Eleanor Roosevelt narrated his "Hello, World!" for RCA Recordings; his work "A Death in the Family" was cited at Kennedy Center as an outstanding new opera. William Mayer is the recipient of Guggenheim and MacDowell fellowships, National Endowment for the Arts' grants, and a Lifetime Achievement citation from the Center for Contemporary Opera, among other honors. With William Mayer was his wife, Meredith.

[7] Through her great-grandparents, Harriet and Sigmund M. Lehman, Terry Asiel is a descendant of both Mayer and Emanuel Lehman.

[8] A graduate of Yale and Oxford, William Bernhard, a son of Dorothy and Richard Bernhard, served for several years in the U.S. Air Force. He is a secretary of the International

Council of the New York Museum of Modern Art. With William Bernhard came his wife, Catherine Cahill.

[9] Cynthia, the daughter of William and Meredith Mayer, is a great-great-granddaughter of Emanuel Lehman. With Cynthia Rubinfien was her husband, Leo.

[10] Charles Chiara is a grandson of John L. Loeb, Sr., and Arthur Lehman's daughter Frances. With Charles Chiara were his wife Renée and their one-year-old son, Julian.

[11] Richard N. Beaty, Jr., is another grandson of John L. Loeb, Sr., and Arthur Lehman's daughter Frances. He was accompanied by his wife, Karin.

[12] Through his great-grandparents, Harriet and Sigmund M. Lehman, Orin McCluskey is a descendant of both Mayer and Emanuel Lehman.

[13] In addition, the group included John L. Loeb's companion, Karen McGowan, and New York editor Louise Stern.

[14] All documents relating to the family reunion were provided by John L. Loeb, Jr.

[15] Robert A. Bernhard, a son of Mayer Lehman's granddaughter Dorothy Bernhard and Richard Bernhard, is a co-owner of the investment management firm Munn, Bernhard Assoc., Inc.; *The Lehman Family Directory 1995,* compiled by Wendy Lehman Lash, edited by Robert A. Klein.

[16] John Langeloth Loeb, Sr., died December 8, 1996, in New York at the age of 94. In an obituary, the *New York Times* called him "a philanthropist who was active in political affairs as well as a pillar of Wall Street's Old Guard." John Loeb supported the presidential campaigns of both Lyndon Johnson and Hubert Humphrey. Over the years, he gave more than 100 million dollars to Harvard University. In his later years, he became a friend of Mayor Teddy Kollek of Jerusalem and financed an Arab community center in East Jerusalem.

[17] Ruth Nelkin (letter to the author, November 12, 1996).

[18] Bötsch specifically mentioned the American presence in Europe after World War II, which had "made it possible for the Western part of our country to grow in accordance with the ideals of Western democracy, the sharing of powers, and human rights."

[19] Roland Flade, *Die Lehmanns und die Rimparer Juden. Zur Dauerausstellung im Rathaus Rimpar,* Würzburg, 1996, pp. 19, 26-29.

[20] Erika Tannenwald (letter to the author, January 6, 1997). The letter contains detailed recollections of Jewish life in Rimpar by her husband Fred (Fritz) Tannenwald and her brother-in-law, Kurt Tannenwald.

[21] Flade, *Die Lehmanns,* pp. 28-29.

[22] Hermann Mündlein, director of the Wirsberg-Gymnasium, spoke on its behalf. Gunter Schönweitz, a teacher at the Wirsberg-Gymnasium and, together with his colleague Herbert Schnell, the driving force behind the exchange program, served as interpreter during the ceremony.

[23] On June 22, 1981, Yehuda Amichai was awarded the Würzburg *Kulturpreis* (award for cultural achievements). The quote is from his acceptance speech. *Main-Post,* June 24, 1981. Amichai's poems, short stories, and his novel *Not of This Time, Not of This Place,* describing a Jewish emigrant's return to Würzburg, are available in English translations. His collection of poems, *Amen,* sold particularly well in the United States. Amichai's name has been mentioned in connection with the Nobel prize for literature.

[24] William Mayer (letter to the author, July 24, 1996).

[25] "Pilgrimage to Lehman home," June 3, 1996.

[26] "Picking up the threads," June 3, 1996.

[27] "Deutsch Treat for Lehman Clan," June 10, 1996.

[28] June 18, 1996.

[29] "A Noted Family Commemorates the Past by Visiting It," June 18, 1996.

[30] "Gedenktafel ehrt Herbert Lehman," June 19, 1996.

[31] John L. Loeb, Jr., "There are no Jews in Rimpar," in *Sentinel,* Chicago, September 12,

1996. The article was also published, among others, in *The Jewish Herald,* August 30, 1996, and *The Arizona Jewish Post,* September 13, 1996. A slightly different version, "Letter from Rimpar: The Echoes Come Back," appeared in *Forward,* New York City, July 19, 1996. In 1998, John Loeb, Jr. was approached by Samuel Leopold Schloss of Montgomery, Alabama, about a possible connection between the Schloss and the Lehman families. It turned out that the grandfather of Samuel Schloss, Leopold Schloss, who had emigrated from Germany to the United States in 1867 at the age of 25, was the son of Abraham Lehmann's first child, Zeira. In 1870, two years after Mayer Lehman had left the city to join his brother Emanuel in New York, Leopold Schloss was working as a grocery clerk in Montgomery. One year later, he started a partnership as Schloss and Kahn, Inc. His son and grandson also worked there. The latter retired in 1994, two years before the company was sold to the Sara Lee Corporation. In his will, dated January 28, 1885, Leopold Schloss mentioned his mother, Charlotte Schloss, in Dieburg, Hesse. She had obviously changed her name from Zeira, as had her sister Babette (formerly Brendel). Also mentioned in the will are Marcus, Leopold's brother, and his sister Adelheid. Both were still living in Germany. In the family tree of the Lehman family, Adelheid's name is abbreviated "Ad" which, in footnote 13 on p. 29, was falsely supposed to mean "Adolf." Samuel Leopold Schloss (letters to the author, January 6, 1999, May 1, 1999).

Appendix
Messages to the Lehman family

The White House
Washington
June 12, 1996

Warm greetings to everyone gathered in Rimpar, Germany, to honor the Lehman family.

Bringing with them little more than their wits, their energy, and their belief in the American Dream, members of the Lehman family emigrated to the United States more than 150 years ago, seeking to make a better life for themselves and their posterity. Since that time, family members have found success in America and have helped to shape its destiny.

Distinguishing themselves as public servants, financiers, humanitarians, and upstanding citizens, members of the Lehman family have contributed much to America's success and have brought honor to their name and to the city of Rimpar. Germans and Americans alike are proud to claim this family as their own, and their ongoing success is a testament to the spirit and values of both our nations.

Best wishes to all for a memorable event.

Bill Clinton

State of New York, Executive Chamber, Albany
George E. Pataki, Governor
June 5, 1996

Dear Friends:

On behalf of the State of New York, it is my great pleasure to offer greetings and congratulations as the light of public recognition shines brightly upon the Lehman family and its descendants. The city of Rimpar, Germany, is to be commended for its gracious hospitality and for hosting ceremonies to honor the Lehman family on June 17, 1996.

As Governor of New York, I am proud to join in the spirit of this occasion as Ambassador John Loeb, Jr., a great-grandson of one of the three brothers who founded Lehman Brothers, proudly heads the distinguished family delegation. The unveiling of a plaque on the house where the three Lehman brothers grew up and the opening of a permanent exhibition in Town Hall featuring the family and commemorating the history of the Jews of Rimpar are certain to be memorable moments for both the Lehman family and their descendants and for the citizens of Rimpar.

It is my hope that this event is a tremendous success. Best wishes to all.

Very truly yours

George E. Pataki

Congregation Emanu-El of the City of New York
Study of the Senior Rabbi
Dr. Ronald D. Sobel
April 19, 1996

My dear John:

I was particularly delighted to learn that the community of Rimpar, Germany, has planned to honor the great Lehman family with special ceremonies on June 17th. The children of Abraham Lehman who came to the New World, and their progeny who followed them, have made monumental contributions to the welfare of the United States and the well-being of the Jewish people all over the world. Therefore, it is altogether fitting that the city from whence the Lehmans came should take this occasion to honor and pay homage to one of the more remarkable families in modern history.

As the Senior Rabbi of Temple Emanu-El in New York City, the largest Jewish House of Worship in the world, I take particular pride, for it was here that members of the Lehman family began to assume leadership roles in the late nineteenth century. Mayer Lehman and his brother, Emanuel, were elected to the Temple's Board of Trustees in the late 1890's. Mayer's son, Judge Irving Lehman, was elected to the same Board in 1919, and served as the Congregation's President from 1929 to 1938. The latter's intellectual interests led him to become a student of ancient and modern Hebraic culture; consequently, he was active throughout his adult life in the promotion of Jewish religious education and cultural programs. Those same interests led him to amass a remarkable collection of Judaic art objects, which were bequeathed to, and remain in the possession of, Temple Emanu-El.

Judge Lehman's brother, Herbert, well-known as Governor of New York and United States Senator, was also deeply involved in Jewish life as a leading figure of the Joint Distribution Committee after World War I. He was also Vice-Chairman of the Palestine Economic Corporation, a Trustee of the Hebrew Sheltering Guardian Society and the Bureau of Jewish Social Research. He retained all his positions with Jewish philanthropic agencies during his long and distinguished public career.

Today, the Lehman tradition continues at Temple Emanu-El, as Robert M. Morgenthau and Robert A. Bernhard serve on the Temple's Board of Trustees. We also take great pleasure in the many years of service that your father, John Loeb, Sr., gave to the Congregation as a member of our Board. And, finally, dear John, we cherish your membership in the Congregation, your great service as Ambassador to Denmark, and your profound commitment to researching the genealogical story of your family.

The Lehman name stands prominent on the topography of American life and the landscape of twentieth century Jewish history.

It all began in Rimpar, so long ago; how fitting and appropriate that there you gather this June to commemorate the history of your family as part of the story of Jewish life in that small German city.

I salute you for the important role that you are playing in making this Commemoration possible.

With deep friendship

Ronald

Federal Republic of Germany
The Chancellor
Bonn
June 1996

I bid the members of the Lehman and Loeb families, who have assembled in Rimpar, a hearty welcome and my best wishes.

I congratulate the citizens of Rimpar on their decision to invite the descendants of Abraham Lehmann, thus setting an example that will be recognized far beyond their village.

By accepting the invitation, the members of the Lehman and Loeb families show their appreciation of the unanimous decision of the municipal council to keep up the memory of Jewish life in Rimpar and the victims of the Holocaust with a plaque and a permanent exhibition in the town hall, right in the center of the village.

Dear members of the Lehman and Loeb families, dear citizens of Rimpar: Today's ceremony is unique. The descendants of a family that left its home one and a half centuries ago congregate in the village where their ancestors had lived and worked for a long time. It is an American family with German-Jewish roots, a family that cherishes the memory of its past in the knowledge that human rights, democracy, and freedom determine Germany's present and future.

Thus, the hours spent together in Rimpar combine reflection and joy.

With my best wishes for a festive family reunion and ceremony I remain
Yours sincerely

Helmut Kohl

Bibliography

Alfons Arnold, *Rimpar im Schein der Fürstenherrlichkeit,* Rimpar, 1965.

Elliott Ashkenazi, *The Business of Jews in Louisiana, 1840-1875,* Tuscaloosa, 1988.

Elliott Ashkenazi, "Jewish Commercial Interests Between North and South: The Case of the Lehmans and the Seligmans," in *American Jewish Archives,* vol. XLIII, No. 1, Spring/Summer 1991.

Avraham Barkai, "German-Jewish Migrations in the Nineteenth Century, 1830-1910," in *Year Book of the Leo Baeck Institute,* vol. 30, 1985.

Hans-Peter Baum, "Jewish Life in Franconia," in *Genizah. Hidden Legacies of the German Village Jews. An Exhibition by The Hidden Legacy Foundation,* Wien, 1992.

Dorothy Bernhard, *Fourth Report, Mayer Lehman Charity Account, June 1, 1941 to June 1, 1942* (Columbia University Libraries, Herbert H. Lehman Suite and Papers).

Stephen Birmingham, *Our Crowd. The Great Jewish Families of New York,* New York, Evanston, and London, 1972.

Harm Hinrich Brandt (ed.), *Zwischen Schutzherrschaft und Emanzipation. Studien zur Geschichte der mainfränkischen Juden im 19. Jahrhundert* (Mainfränkische Studien, vol. 39), Würzburg, 1987.

A Centennial. Lehman Brothers 1850-1950, New York, 1950.

Leonard Dinnerstein, *America and the Survivors of the Holocaust,* New York, 1982.

Roland Flade, *Juden in Würzburg, 1918-1933* (Mainfränkische Studien, vol. 34), Würzburg (2nd edition), 1986.

Roland Flade, *Der Novemberpogrom von 1938 in Unterfranken. Vorgeschichte, Verlauf, Augenzeugenberichte* (Schriften des Stadtarchivs Würzburg, vol. 6), Würzburg, 1988.

Roland Flade, *Die Würzburger Juden. Ihre Geschichte vom Mittelalter bis zur Gegenwart. Mit einem Beitrag von Ursula Gehring-Münzel,* Würzburg, 1987.

Eric Foner, *Reconstruction. America's Unfinished Revolution, 1863-1877,* New York, 1989.

Ursula Gehring-Münzel, *Vom Schutzjuden zum Staatsbürger. Die gesellschaftliche Integration der Würzburger Juden 1803-1871* (Veröffentlichungen des Stadtarchivs Würzburg, vol. 6), Würzburg, 1992.

Ursula Gehring-Münzel, "Emanzipation," in Flade, *Würzburger Juden,* S. 61-141.

Robert Gellately, *The Gestapo and German Society. Enforcing Racial Policy 1933-1945,* Oxford, 1990.

Rudolf Glanz, "The German-Jewish Mass Emigration 1820-1880," in *American Jewish Archives,* vol. 22, April 1970.

Rudolf Glanz, "The Immigration of German Jews up to 1880," in *Yivo Annual of Jewish Social Sciences,* vol. 2-3, New York, 1947.

Richard Glazar, *Die Falle mit dem grünen Zaun. Überleben in Treblinka,* Frankfurt am Main, 1992.

Edwin Hamberger, *Das fürstliche Landschloß zu Rimpar im 17. und 18. Jahrhundert* (Mainfränkische Studien, vol. 41), Würzburg, 1987.

James F. Harris, *The People Speak! Anti-Semitism and Emancipation in Nineteenth-Century Bavaria,* Ann Arbor, 1994.

In Memoriam. Mayer Lehman. New York, 1897.

Weymouth T. Jordan, *Ante-Bellum Alabama. Town and Country. With an Introduction by Kenneth R. Johnson,* Tallahassee, Fla., 1957.

Jacob Katz, *Out of the Ghetto. The Social Background of Jewish Emancipation, 1770-1870,* Cambridge, Mass., 1973.

Jacob Katz, *Die Hep-Hep-Verfolgungen des Jahres 1819,* Berlin, 1994.

Walter H. Kaufman, "A History of the Jewish Teachers Seminary in Würzburg (ILBA)," in Max Ottensoser, Alex Roberg (eds.), *ILBA. Israelitische Lehrerbildungsanstalt Würzburg, 1864-1938, by the Alumni of 1930-1938,* Huntington Woods, Michigan, 1982.

Bertram Wallace Korn, "Jews and Negro Slavery in the Old South, 1789-1865," in Leonard Dinnerstein, Mary Dale Palsson (eds.), *Jews in the South,* Baton Rouge, 1973.

Gisela Krug, "Die Juden in Mainfranken zu Beginn des 19. Jahrhunderts. Statistische Untersuchungen zu ihrer sozialen und wirtschaftlichen Situation," in Brandt (ed.), *Schutzherrschaft.*

Henry S. Marks, *Past Jewish Life in Alabama* (unpublished manuscript).

Henry S. Marks, Marsha Kass Marks, "Jewish Life in Alabama: The Formative Stages," in *Alabama Heritage,* vol. 36, Spring 1995.

Henry Morgenthau III, *Mostly Morgenthaus: A Family History. With a Foreword by Arthur Schlesinger, Jr.,* New York, 1991.

Allan Nevins, *Herbert H. Lehman and His Era,* New York, 1963.

Baruch Zvi Ophir, Falk Wiesemann (eds.), *Die jüdischen Gemeinden in Bayern 1918-1945. Geschichte und Zerstörung,* München, Wien, 1979.

H. G. Reissner, "The German-American Jews (1800-1850)," in *Year Book of the Leo Baeck Institute,* vol. 10, 1965.

The Reminiscences of Herbert H. Lehman, Oral History Research Office, Columbia University, New York, 1961, 1969.

Karl-Thomas Remlein, "Der Bayerische Landtag und die Judenemanzipation nach der Revolution 1848," in Brandt (ed.), *Schutzherrschaft.*

Howard M. Sachar, *A History of Israel. From the Rise of Zionism to Our Time,* New York, 1979.

Jutta Sporck-Pfitzer, *Die ehemaligen jüdischen Gemeinden im Landkreis Würzburg,* Würzburg, 1988.

Reiner Strätz, *Biographisches Handbuch Würzburger Juden 1900-1945,* Würzburg, 1989.

Oscar Salomon Straus, *Under Four Administrations. From Cleveland to Taft,* Boston, New York, 1922.

Herbert A. Strauss, "Jewish Emigration from Germany. Nazi Policies and Jewish Responses (I)," in *Year Book of the Leo Baeck Institute*, vol. 25, 1980.

Herbert A. Strauss, "Jewish Emigration from Germany. Nazi Policies and Jewish Responses (II)," in *Year Book of the Leo Baeck Institute*, vol. 26, 1981.

Jacob Toury, "Jewish Manual Labour and Emigration. Records from some Bavarian Districts (1830-1857)," in *Year Book of the Leo Baeck Institute*, vol. 16, 1971.

United States War Dept., Series II, *The War of the Rebellion*, vol. 7, 8.

Mack Walker, *Germany and the Emigration 1816-1885,* Cambridge, Mass., 1964.

Juliane Wetzel, *Jüdisches Leben in München, 1945-1951. Durchgangsstation oder Wiederaufbau?* (Miscellanea Bavarica Monacensia, vol. 135), München, 1987.

Christian Will, Werner Siegler, *Das ist Rimpar. Das Arbeiterdorf vor den Toren der Stadt Würzburg,* Rimpar, 1978.

George Woodbridge, *UNRRA: The History of the United Nations Relief and Rehabilitation Administration,* New York, 1950.

Klaus Wust, Heinz Moos (eds.), *Dreihundert Jahre deutsche Einwanderer in Nordamerika. 1683-1983. Ihre Beiträge zum Werden der Neuen Welt,* Gräfelfing (2nd edition), 1983.

David S. Wyman, *The Abandonment of the Jews. America and the Holocaust, 1941-1945,* New York, 1984.

Leopold Young, *A Sketch of the First Jewish Settlers of Montgomery, and a Short History of Kahl Montgomery* (typewritten manuscript), Montgomery, 1900.

Index

Abraham, Henry, 68
Abraham Löw. *See* Lehmann,
    Abraham
Adler, Justin, 98
Alabama, 7, 43-45, 47, 55, 56, 64, 65,
    67, 68, 76
Alabama River, 44, 45
Alabama Warehouse, 63, 65
Albany, New York, 87, 132
Allgemeine Zeitung des Judentums,
    38, 40
Altschul, Arthur G., 9, 59
Altschul, Edith. *See* Lehman, Edith
Altschul, Frank, 59
Altschul, Helen (Lehman), 59, 71
American Express, 115
American Federation of Labor, 87,
    105
American Friends of the Hebrew
    University in Jerusalem, 89
Amichai, Yehuda, 127
Amsterdam, 48
Ansbacher, Minna, 101, 103
Ansbacher, Mordechai, 101, 103
Antwerp, 48
Appomattox Court House, 65
Arkansas, 43
Aschaffenburg, Bavaria, 110
Ashkenazi, Elliott, 9, 56, 60, 63
Asiel, Terry, 120
Atlantic and Danville Railway
    Company, 88
Auburn, New York, 86
Augsburg, Bavaria, 70
Auschwitz, 8, 125
Austerlitz, 23
Australia, 98, 109
Austria, 23, 94, 95, 109, 110

Austro-Hungarian Empire, 16

Bad Brückenau, Bavaria, 93
Bad Kissingen, Bavaria, 27, 101, 129
Baden, 50
Baiersdorf, Bavaria, 39
Baltimore, 38, 40, 46, 76
Bamberg, Bavaria, 77
Bamberger, Seligmann Bär, 36
Bamberger, Siegfried, 98
Bank of England, 129
Barcelona, 48
Bavaria, 7, 8, 18, 23, 25, 26, 28, 29,
    33, 35, 37-39, 43, 44-46, 50, 51,
    53, 60, 79, 90, 111, 126, 128
Bavarian State Archives, Würzburg, 7,
    8, 24
Beaty, Karin, 128, 130
Beaty, Richard N., Jr., 120
Beelitz, Frank, 126, 127
Beer, Sara. *See* Newgass, Sara
Bein, Clara. *See* Schwab, Clara
Bein, Hugo, 98
Belgium, 107
Ben-Gurion, David, 111
Bergen Brunswig, 66
Berlin, 50, 90, 98, 115
Bernhard, Dorothy (Lehman), 95-97,
    129, 130
Bernhard, Richard, 129, 130
Bernhard, Robert A., 122, 133
Bernhard, William, 120, 120, 130
Beverly Hills, 113
Bing, Abraham, 29, 33, 36
Birmingham, Stephen, 38, 59
Black, Hugo, 66
Black Sea, 84, 107
Bloomingdale, Joseph, 39
Bloomingdale, Lyman, 39
Bloomingdale Brothers Department
    Store, 39
Blumenthal, Benjamin, 39
Bonn, 50, 126, 134

Lehmann, Samuel, 12, 26, 63
Lehmann, Seligmann, 12, 25, 44, 45,
    51, 53, 63, 69, 73, 81, 82, 97, 99,
    100, 129
Lehmann, Zeira. *See* Schloss,
    Charlotte
Lepis, Cabrini B., 9
Lewisohn, Adele. *See* Lehman, Adele
Lewisohn, Adolph, 77
Leymeister, Ignatz, 33
Liberal Democratic Party, 119, 120,
    129
Limburg, Clara (Lehman), 70, 71, 77,
    78, 100
Limburg, Richard, 77
Lincoln, Abraham, 50, 60, 62, 65
Link, Wendell, 80
Lisbon, 97
Lithuania, 110
Liverpool, 9, 34, 35, 68, 70, 77, 79
Liverpool Cotton Exchange, 77
Loeb, Ann, 117
Loeb family, 134
Loeb, Frances Lehman, 77, 128-130
Loeb, John L., 77, 122, 129, 130, 134
Loeb, John L., Jr., 7, 8, 77, 116-125,
    127, 128, 132-134
Loeb, Rhoades, 77, 116
Lohr, Bavaria, 77, 110
London, 9, 34, 35, 50, 70, 77, 79, 81,
    118, 119
London School of Economics, 129
Long Island, 119
Lonnerstädter, Siegfried, 98
Los Angeles, 70
Louisiana, 9, 76
Louisville, Kentucky, 63
Löw, Abraham. *See* Lehmann,
    Abraham
Löw, Seligmann, 11-18, 21, 22, 25, 31,
    32, 34, 45, 82, 116
Lower Franconia, 7, 32, 39, 41, 46,

47, 51, 53, 57, 73, 87, 90-93,
    102, 110-112, 125

Macy, R. H., & Co., 76
Madison Square Garden, 91, 102
Main-Post, 7
Main River, 13, 16, 38, 41
Maine, 43
Mainz, 39, 41, 78
Manhattan, 43, 56, 70
Marion, Alabama, 47
Marks, Henry S., 9
Massachusetts, 81
Matrikelparagraph, 26, 37, 51, 79
Matthias-Ehrenfried-Schule, Rimpar,
    126
Max of Bavaria, Duke, 126, 128
Maximilian II, king of Bavaria, 51
Maximilian-Kolbe-Schule, Rimpar,
    126
Mayer Lehman Charity Fund, 95-97,
    101, 118
Mayer und Babette Lehmann-
    Wohltätigkeitsstiftung, 81
Mayer, Meredith, 129
Mayer, William, 120, 127, 129
McAuliffe, Sharon, 82
McCarthy, Joseph, 114
McCloy, John, 77
McCluskey, Orin, 120, 125
McGowan, Karen, 130
Meany, George, 87
Meier Lesser, 11, 12, 15, 18, 26, 82,
    87
Memphis, Tennessee, 74
Metropolitan Museum of Art, New
    York, 7, 115, 116, 129
Miami, Florida, 96
Michelbacher, Maximilian, 60
Michigan, 43
Minnesota, 113
Mississippi, 60
Mississippi River, 39

Roosevelt, Franklin D., 59, 66, 84-87, 94, 102, 106, 107, 111
Rosenbaum, Mendel, 53
Rosenbaum, Peggy. *See* Lehman, Peggy
Rosenheim, Adelheid, 35
Rosenheim, Babette, daughter of Seligmann Löw, 18, 32, 34
Rosenheim, Babette, daughter of Moritz Rosenheim, 35
Rosenheim, Betty, daughter of Moritz Rosenheim, 35
Rosenheim, Betty, daughter of Samuel Rosenheim, 34
Rosenheim, Edel, 11-13, 18, 21, 31-34, 82
Rosenheim family, 36, 37, 70
Rosenheim, Felix, 77
Rosenheim, Hedwig (Hellmann), 35
Rosenheim, Hermann, 35
Rosenheim, Jeanette (Nanny Dunkelspiel), 34
Rosenheim, Johanna, 34
Rosenheim, Joseph, son of Seligmann Löw, 18, 32, 34, 122
Rosenheim, Joseph, son of Leopold Rosenheim, 35, 70, 77
Rosenheim, Julius, 35
Rosenheim, Klara (Dunkelspiel), 18, 32, 34
Rosenheim, L., & Sons, 70, 77
Rosenheim, Lina, 35
Rosenheim, Löw (Leopold), 18, 32, 33, 35, 70
Rosenheim, Max, son of Joseph Rosenheim, 35
Rosenheim, Max, son of Moritz Rosenheim, 35
Rosenheim, Meier, 35
Rosenheim, Mina (Segnitz), 33
Rosenheim, Moises (Moritz), son of Seligmann Löw, 18, 32-34

Rosenheim, Moritz, son of Joseph Rosenheim, 35
Rosenheim, Philippine (Kahn), 34
Rosenheim, Samuel, 18, 32-34
Rosenheim, Seligmann, son of Leopold Rosenheim, 35
Rosenheim, Seligmann, son of Samuel Rosenheim, 34
Rosenheim, Sigmund, son of Joseph Rosenheim, 35
Rosenheim, Sigmund, son of Moritz Rosenheim, 35
Rosenheim, Theodor, 35
Rosenheim, Wilhelm, 35
Rosenthal, Jonas, 98
Rosenwald, Edith. *See* Stern, Edith
Rosenwald, Julius, 69
Rothschild, Heinrich, 98
Rotschild, N., 30
Rotschild, Rahel. *See* Schwab, Rahel
Rotterdam, 41, 46, 48
Royal Air Force, 110
Rubinfien, Cynthia, 120
Rubinfien, Leo, 129
Ruland, Dr. Anton, 51
Rumania, 107, 109
Russia, 23, 83, 102, 104, 109, 110

Sachs Collegiate Institute, New York, 46, 81
Sachs, Joseph, 46
Sachs, Julius, 46
Sachs, Sam, 46
St. Petersburg, 48
Saltman, Adelheid. *See* Schwab, Adelheid
Salzburg, 23
San Francisco, 70, 77
Sara Lee Corporation, 131
Savannah, Georgia, 46
Schiff, Jacob, 115
Schloss and Kahn, Inc., 131
Schloss, Adelheid, 29, 131

What the critics said about *The Lehmans:*

"A remarkable book."
– *Handelsblatt, Germany's leading business newspaper*

"*[The Lehmans]* is full of fascinating material and goes a long way in reinforcing emphasis on the transatlantic connections among the unusual group of German (mostly Bavarian) Jews who became so influential in the international banking community by the last quarter of the 19th century."
– *Elliott Ashkenazi, author of "The Business of Jews in Louisiana, 1840-1875"*

"A highly interesting study, thoroughly researched. It captivates the reader."
– *Das Historisch-Politische Buch*

"An important contribution, and a rare example of a family history of this type coming from a German researcher."
– *Karen S. Franklin, Director, Family Research Program, Leo Baeck Institute, New York*

"Sheds new light on the [Lehman] family." *- The Jewish Chronicle, Pittsburgh*

By the same author:

Die Würzburger Juden. Ihre Geschichte vom Mittelalter bis zur Gegenwart

Mit einem Beitrag von Ursula Gehring-Münzel

Second edition 1996, 469 pp., many illustrations

"Probably the most thorough and most readable book dealing with the Jews of a medium-sized city."
– *Aufbau. America's only German-Jewish publication*

"Among the many histories of Jews in German cities and regions, this volume stands out by virtue of its readability and attractive format. The emphasis is on individuals, and the more general account is enriched by personal documents."
– *Shofar, Book Review Section, Purdue University, West Lafayette, Indiana*

"The book covers in detail all aspects of Jewish communal, social, and economic life ... and deals also with many Jewish personalities active in Jewish or general public affairs."
– *Year Book of the Leo Baeck Institute*

Königshausen & Neumann
P.O.B. 6007 - D-97010 Würzburg - Germany